Three Jade Life Star

Feng Shui Essentials: Xuan Kong Life Star
THREE JADE LIFE STAR

Copyright © 2011 by Joey Yap
All rights reserved worldwide.
Second Edition January 2013

All intellectual property rights contained or in relation to this book belongs to Joey Yap.

No part of this book may be copied, used, subsumed, or exploited in fact, field of thought or general idea, by any other authors or persons, or be stored in a retrieval system, transmitted or reproduced in any way, including but not limited to digital copying and printing in any form whatsoever worldwide without the prior agreement and written permission of the author.

The author can be reached at:

Mastery Academy of Chinese Metaphysics Sdn. Bhd. (611143-A)
19-3, The Boulevard, Mid Valley City,
59200 Kuala Lumpur, Malaysia.
Tel   : +603-2284 8080
Fax   : +603-2284 1218
Website : www.masteryacademy.com

DISCLAIMER:

The author, Joey Yap and the publisher, JY Books Sdn Bhd, have made their best efforts to produce this high quality, informative and helpful book. They have verified the technical accuracy of the information and contents of this book. Any information pertaining to the events, occurrences, dates and other details relating to the person or persons, dead or alive, and to the companies have been verified to the best of their abilities based on information obtained or extracted from various websites, newspaper clippings and other public media. However, they make no representation or warranties of any kind with regard to the contents of this book and accept no liability of any kind for any losses or damages caused or alleged to be caused directly or indirectly from using the information contained herein.

Published by JY Books Sdn. Bhd. (659134-T)

Table of content :

1	**LIFE STAR REFERENCE TABLE**	7
2	**INTRODUCTION**	12
3	**YOUR XUAN KONG LIFE STAR**	23
	Basic Attributes	24
4	**YOUR FENG SHUI ESSENTIALS**	27
	Directions	29
	Taking the Direction using a Compass	33
	Favorable Directions	39
	Unfavorable Directions	49
	Bed Alignment Direction	58
	Best Floor	60
	Personal Grand Duke Direction	65
	Personal Clash Direction	71
	Flying Star Effects	76
5	**THE FIVE ELEMENT**	97

6	**CHARACTERISTICS OF STAR**	109
	The Good	111
	The Bad	117
7	**CAREER AND WEALTH**	123
	Characteristics at work	124
	Suitable Job Roles	128
	Career and Wealth Guide	132
8	**RELATIONSHIPS**	139
	Guide for Relationships	140
9	**HEALTH**	145
	Guide for Health	146
10	**COMPATIBILITY with OTHER LIFE STARS**	151

LIFE STAR REFERENCE TABLE

Year Pillar and Gua Number Reference Table for 1912 - 2055

Animal	Year of Birth			Gua Number for Male	Gua Number for Female	Year of Birth			Gua Number for Male	Gua Number for Female
Rat	1912	壬子 Ren Zi	Water Rat	7	8	1936	丙子 Bing Zi	Fire Rat	1	5
Ox	1913	癸丑 Gui Chou	Water Ox	6	9	1937	丁丑 Ding Chou	Fire Ox	9	6
Tiger	1914	甲寅 Jia Yin	Wood Tiger	5	1	1938	戊寅 Wu Yin	Earth Tiger	8	7
Rabbit	1915	乙卯 Yi Mao	Wood Rabbit	4	2	1939	己卯 Ji Mao	Earth Rabbit	7	8
Dragon	1916	丙辰 Bing Chen	Fire Dragon	3	3	1940	庚辰 Geng Chen	Metal Dragon	6	9
Snake	1917	丁巳 Ding Si	Fire Snake	2	4	1941	辛巳 Xin Si	Metal Snake	5	1
Horse	1918	戊午 Wu Wu	Earth Horse	1	5	1942	壬午 Ren Wu	Water Horse	4	2
Goat	1919	己未 Ji Wei	Earth Goat	9	6	1943	癸未 Gui Wei	Water Goat	3	3
Monkey	1920	庚申 Geng Shen	Metal Monkey	8	7	1944	甲申 Jia Shen	Wood Monkey	2	4
Rooster	1921	辛酉 Xin You	Metal Rooster	7	8	1945	乙酉 Yi You	Wood Rooster	1	5
Dog	1922	壬戌 Ren Xu	Water Dog	6	9	1946	丙戌 Bing Xu	Fire Dog	9	6
Pig	1923	癸亥 Gui Hai	Water Pig	5	1	1947	丁亥 Ding Hai	Fire Pig	8	7
Rat	1924	甲子 Jia Zi	Wood Rat	4	2	1948	戊子 Wu Zi	Earth Rat	7	8
Ox	1925	乙丑 Yi Chou	Wood Ox	3	3	1949	己丑 Ji Chou	Earth Ox	6	9
Tiger	1926	丙寅 Bing Yin	Fire Tiger	2	4	1950	庚寅 Geng Yin	Metal Tiger	5	1
Rabbit	1927	丁卯 Ding Mao	Fire Rabbit	1	5	1951	辛卯 Xin Mao	Metal Rabbit	4	2
Dragon	1928	戊辰 Wu Chen	Earth Dragon	9	6	1952	壬辰 Ren Chen	Water Dragon	3	3
Snake	1929	己巳 Ji Si	Earth Snake	8	7	1953	癸巳 Gui Si	Water Snake	2	4
Horse	1930	庚午 Geng Wu	Metal Horse	7	8	1954	甲午 Jia Wu	Wood Horse	1	5
Goat	1931	辛未 Xin Wei	Metal Goat	6	9	1955	乙未 Yi Wei	Wood Goat	9	6
Monkey	1932	壬申 Ren Shen	Water Monkey	5	1	1956	丙申 Bing Shen	Fire Monkey	8	7
Rooster	1933	癸酉 Gui You	Water Rooster	4	2	1957	丁酉 Ding You	Fire Rooster	7	8
Dog	1934	甲戌 Jia Xu	Wood Dog	3	3	1958	戊戌 Wu Xu	Earth Dog	6	9
Pig	1935	乙亥 Yi Hai	Wood Pig	2	4	1959	己亥 Ji Hai	Earth Pig	5	1

- Please note that the date for the Chinese Solar Year starts on Feb 4. This means that if you were born in Feb 2 of 2002, you belong to the previous year 2001.

Year Pillar and Gua Number Reference Table for 1912 - 2055

Animal	Year of Birth			Gua Number for Male	Gua Number for Female	Year of Birth			Gua Number for Male	Gua Number for Female
Rat	1960	庚子 Geng Zi	Metal Rat	4	2	1984	甲子 Jia Zi	Wood Rat	7	8
Ox	1961	辛丑 Xin Chou	Metal Ox	3	3	1985	乙丑 Yi Chou	Wood Ox	6	9
Tiger	1962	壬寅 Ren Yin	Water Tiger	2	4	1986	丙寅 Bing Yin	Fire Tiger	5	1
Rabbit	1963	癸卯 Gui Mao	Water Rabbit	1	5	1987	丁卯 Ding Mao	Fire Rabbit	4	2
Dragon	1964	甲辰 Jia Chen	Wood Dragon	9	6	1988	戊辰 Wu Chen	Earth Dragon	3	3
Snake	1965	乙巳 Yi Si	Wood Snake	8	7	1989	己巳 Ji Si	Earth Snake	2	4
Horse	1966	丙午 Bing Wu	Fire Horse	7	8	1990	庚午 Geng Wu	Metal Horse	1	5
Goat	1967	丁未 Ding Wei	Fire Goat	6	9	1991	辛未 Xin Wei	Metal Goat	9	6
Monkey	1968	戊申 Wu Shen	Earth Monkey	5	1	1992	壬申 Ren Shen	Water Monkey	8	7
Rooster	1969	己酉 Ji You	Earth Rooster	4	2	1993	癸酉 Gui You	Water Rooster	7	8
Dog	1970	庚戌 Geng Xu	Metal Dog	3	3	1994	甲戌 Jia Xu	Wood Dog	6	9
Pig	1971	辛亥 Xin Hai	Metal Pig	2	4	1995	乙亥 Yi Hai	Wood Pig	5	1
Rat	1972	壬子 Ren Zi	Water Rat	1	5	1996	丙子 Bing Zi	Fire Rat	4	2
Ox	1973	癸丑 Gui Chou	Water Ox	9	6	1997	丁丑 Ding Chou	Fire Ox	3	3
Tiger	1974	甲寅 Jia Yin	Wood Tiger	8	7	1998	戊寅 Wu Yin	Earth Tiger	2	4
Rabbit	1975	乙卯 Yi Mao	Wood Rabbit	7	8	1999	己卯 Ji Mao	Earth Rabbit	1	5
Dragon	1976	丙辰 Bing Chen	Fire Dragon	6	9	2000	庚辰 Geng Chen	Metal Dragon	9	6
Snake	1977	丁巳 Ding Si	Fire Snake	5	1	2001	辛巳 Xin Si	Metal Snake	8	7
Horse	1978	戊午 Wu Wu	Earth Horse	4	2	2002	壬午 Ren Wu	Water Horse	7	8
Goat	1979	己未 Ji Wei	Earth Goat	3	3	2003	癸未 Gui Wei	Water Goat	6	9
Monkey	1980	庚申 Geng Shen	Metal Monkey	2	4	2004	甲申 Jia Shen	Wood Monkey	5	1
Rooster	1981	辛酉 Xin You	Metal Rooster	1	5	2005	乙酉 Yi You	Wood Rooster	4	2
Dog	1982	壬戌 Ren Xu	Water Dog	9	6	2006	丙戌 Bing Xu	Fire Dog	3	3
Pig	1983	癸亥 Gui Hai	Water Pig	8	7	2007	丁亥 Ding Hai	Fire Pig	2	4

- Please note that the date for the Chinese Solar Year starts on Feb 4. This means that if you were born in Feb 2 of 2002, you belong to the previous year 2001.

Year Pillar and Gua Number Reference Table for 1912 - 2055

Animal	Year of Birth			Gua Number for Male	Gua Number for Female	Year of Birth			Gua Number for Male	Gua Number for Female
Rat	2008	戊子 Wu Zi	Earth Rat	1	5	2032	壬子 Ren Zi	Water Rat	4	2
Ox	2009	己丑 Ji Chou	Earth Ox	9	6	2033	癸丑 Gui Chou	Water Ox	3	3
Tiger	2010	庚寅 Geng Yin	Metal Tiger	8	7	2034	甲寅 Jia Yin	Wood Tiger	2	4
Rabbit	2011	辛卯 Xin Mao	Metal Rabbit	7	8	2035	乙卯 Yi Mao	Wood Rabbit	1	5
Dragon	2012	壬辰 Ren Chen	Water Dragon	6	9	2036	丙辰 Bing Chen	Fire Dragon	9	6
Snake	2013	癸巳 Gui Si	Water Snake	5	1	2037	丁巳 Ding Si	Fire Snake	8	7
Horse	2014	甲午 Jia Wu	Wood Horse	4	2	2038	戊午 Wu Wu	Earth Horse	7	8
Goat	2015	乙未 Yi Wei	Wood Goat	3	3	2039	己未 Ji Wei	Earth Goat	6	9
Monkey	2016	丙申 Bing Shen	Fire Monkey	2	4	2040	庚申 Geng Shen	Metal Monkey	5	1
Rooster	2017	丁酉 Ding You	Fire Rooster	1	5	2041	辛酉 Xin You	Metal Rooster	4	2
Dog	2018	戊戌 Wu Xu	Earth Dog	9	6	2042	壬戌 Ren Xu	Water Dog	3	3
Pig	2019	己亥 Ji Hai	Earth Pig	8	7	2043	癸亥 Gui Hai	Water Pig	2	4
Rat	2020	庚子 Geng Zi	Metal Rat	7	8	2044	甲子 Jia Zi	Wood Rat	1	5
Ox	2021	辛丑 Xin Chou	Metal Ox	6	9	2045	乙丑 Yi Chou	Wood Ox	9	6
Tiger	2022	壬寅 Ren Yin	Water Tiger	5	1	2046	丙寅 Bing Yin	Fire Tiger	8	7
Rabbit	2023	癸卯 Gui Mao	Water Rabbit	4	2	2047	丁卯 Ding Mao	Fire Rabbit	7	8
Dragon	2024	甲辰 Jia Chen	Wood Dragon	3	3	2048	戊辰 Wu Chen	Earth Dragon	6	9
Snake	2025	乙巳 Yi Si	Wood Snake	2	4	2049	己巳 Ji Si	Earth Snake	5	1
Horse	2026	丙午 Bing Wu	Fire Horse	1	5	2050	庚午 Geng Wu	Metal Horse	4	2
Goat	2027	丁未 Ding Wei	Fire Goat	9	6	2051	辛未 Xin Wei	Metal Goat	3	3
Monkey	2028	戊申 Wu Shen	Earth Monkey	8	7	2052	壬申 Ren Shen	Water Monkey	2	4
Rooster	2029	己酉 Ji You	Earth Rooster	7	8	2053	癸酉 Gui You	Water Rooster	1	5
Dog	2030	庚戌 Geng Xu	Metal Dog	6	9	2054	甲戌 Jia Xu	Wood Dog	9	6
Pig	2031	辛亥 Xin Hai	Metal Pig	5	1	2055	乙亥 Yi Hai	Wood Pig	8	7

- Please note that the date for the Chinese Solar Year starts on Feb 4. This means that if you were born in Feb 2 of 2002, you belong to the previous year 2001.

To download your Three Jade Life Star Reference Chart FREE go to

www.masteryacademy.com/regbook

Here is your unique code for access:

GBSN6013

Introduction

When all is said and done, Feng Shui is the study of how environments affect the people living within them. It can yield advice on which environments, at both a macro and micro level, are 'good' places or 'bad' places to live for given people at given times.

Xuan Kong is only one subsection of the study of Feng Shui and the Life Stars are only one component in the Xuan Kong Feng Shui system. This means that the study of Life Stars gives us only one piece of the overall Feng Shui puzzle but it is an important one!

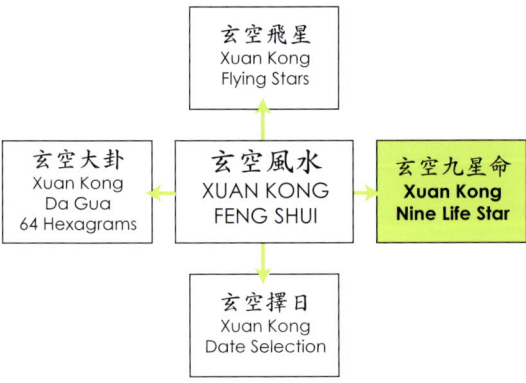

We can use the Xuan Kong Life Star system to help us with a number of practical Feng Shui and interpersonal decisions that make a big impact.

When we assess Feng Shui, we assess four factors: Environment, Buildings, Time and People. This book has been written to complement a number of other Feng Shui titles;

1. *Feng Shui for Homebuyers – Exterior;*
2. *Feng Shui for Homebuyers – Interior;*
3. *Feng Shui for Apartment Buyers;* and
4. *Pure Feng Shui.*

These other books talk about the influence of Environment, Buildings and Time on Feng Shui. This book looks at the final aspect: **People.**

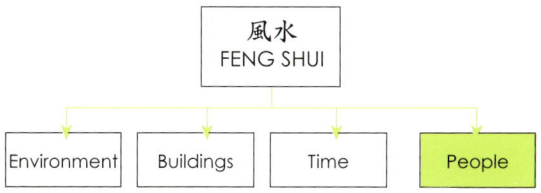

Different people will be affected in different ways by any given environment. The Life Stars directly determine what role the environment plays in the lives of its occupants. Every person is governed by one of the 9 Life Stars. These Stars also help determine key personal characteristics.

In this book, you will learn how the annually changing Xuan Kong Flying Stars interact with your Life Star so that you know what different sectors of your home will bring you. You can then use this information for your own benefit and safety. For maximum benefit, people should seek to align themselves with the direction in their home that yields positive effects. For instance, the #9 Purple Flying Star brings about the potential of career advancement for Star 1 people. Clearly this is a benefit that professionally minded people would like to take advantage of, so they may wish to spend more time absorbing the influence of the #9 Purple Flying Star in their home or place of work. The same Flying Star also indicates a heightened risk of miscarriage for pregnant women though and so pregnant Life Star 1 women should be exercise heightened caution in the presence of this Flying Star, and avoid its influence if possible.

Because the advice generated by this book on Xuan Kong Life Stars takes into account your Life Star when discussing the effects of the Flying Stars, the advice given is highly tailored to your life.

The Positive Side Of You

Your Life Star brings a force to bear on you, wherever you are. This force can have positive or negative effects, depending on the Feng Shui of the environment you reside in.

We are all multi faceted and complex. We have good habits and bad habits; a strong side and a weak side. By correctly tapping into the right Qi your best side will manifest itself more. When you put your best foot forward more in life, more opportunities

and success comes your way. Conversely, if you find yourself under the negative influence of your Life Star, more of your negative personality traits will prevail. Your environment filters out the good or the bad influence of your Life Star. Xuan Kong Feng Shui shows us how we can align ourself to receive the best possible influence. By simply aligning your bed and study desk to correspond with your favourable Personal Directions for example, you can already take one big step towards absorbing the beneficial influence of your Life Star, even whilst you sleep and study! If you are choosing a new home then choosing the correct floor at the correct time will bring further benefits. Avoiding your Personal Grand Duke and Crash Sectors will keep health problems and conflict at bay.

Does all of this mean you must tip-toe around certain rooms in your house or seal them off? No. Feng Shui does not need to become all consuming. If you can easily align your bed so that you receive benefits then why not do so? There are real world limits to what can be done, it is not practical, for instance, to rebuild your home if it does not perfectly cater to the instructions that this book gives. Your ideal floor choice in a condominium may not be available. The list of real world complications goes on.

You can tailor Feng Shui to work for you; making smaller, simple changes so that you reap the maximum possible benefit. The pursuit of good Feng Shui is not intended to take up all of your time and this flexible book is perfect for anyone, no matter how busy or restricted you are in your decisions.

Your Life Star

Everyone falls under the jurisdiction of one of the 9 Life Stars and this will have different consequences for everyone. Your Life Star describes your key skills, characteristics and traits. Some people are creative but reserved, some people are aggressive and driven. What self destructive traits do you have? Do you have a bloated sense of pride or are you prone to gossip? Your Life Star can shine some light on the complexity of your personality and your good and bad traits.

Study of the Life Stars has practical benefits for everyone; it gives you valuable information about others in addition to yourself. Different Life Stars bestow different abilities on people which means that people belonging to each Star will exhibit different characteristics at work. A Star 1 person is diplomatic so they are best suited to roles demanding diplomacy, for example. Accordingly, employers can study the Xuan Kong Life Stars when making work place decisions whilst employees can use the system to help them go about working productively with their colleagues and superiors, even when disagreements arise.

If you become aware of your own harmful tendencies then you can learn to minimize them so you can advance. Similar benefits can be seen in romantic relationships and friendships. Learning that a Star 7 individual needs their space and independence

might help you accommodate this in your dealings with them when you might otherwise have been tempted to be clingy and dependant.

When we understand more about ourselves we can stop ourselves from making mistakes and perhaps forgive certain behaviour in others once we understand where it comes from.

Compatibility Guide

Certain people are, of course, more compatible with each other than others. In partnerships or relationships this takes on a new level of importance. Different Life Stars bestow the qualities of different elements on different people; for example, a Star 1 person has the qualities of water whilst a Star 7 person has the qualities of the Yin Metal element. Just as the elements control, pacify and weaken one another, individuals of the different Stars may dominate, clash with or enrich one another. This book includes a write up of how compatible different Stars are with one another. You may find that a relationship as a Star 1 person with a Star 5 person simply isn't worth the effort. A compatibility guide on each interaction gives you tips on how to best deal with the other Stars for mutual benefit, even taking into account your differences.

Compatible With BaZi Profiling Systems

If you are familiar with the **BaZi Profiling System** then you will be aware that, at first glance, it seems to deal with very similar issues. It can tell us about other preferences and internal view of the world. Do we have an optimistic view of things? Do we blame ourselves too much?

While there is some overlap between the jurisdiction of the Xuan Kong Life Star system and BaZi Profiling System, they are two different systems. They both deal with individual people and their personalities but they are not mutually exclusive. In fact, when studied together, they can be thought of as two pieces of the same puzzle.

The BaZi Profiling System tells us about ourselves and about others. It even tells us things that cannot be observed about others (things people do not communicate). What it can't tell us is how the outside environment plays into the picture. The Xuan Kong Nine Stars help determine *which* qualities are brought out and by what features and external forms in the environment.

Once we know what directions are conducive to good Qi, how external forms (pylons etc) can compound problems related to sectors in the home, which areas of our environment increase the risk of which ailments or even which people can create problems in our lives (compatibility guide) then we can begin shaping our external environment to whatever degree necessary in order to enjoy

the most happiness, wealth and success. Xuan Kong Feng Shui tells you precisely what effect the environment and compass directions will have on which people.

If you are simply interested in learning what makes a person tick rather than making decisions about an ideal environment for them to thrive in then I recommend you take up further study of the BaZi Profiling System. The goal of BaZi is to pinpoint personal deficiencies so that they may be overcome or to highlight personal strengths so that they may be capitalised on.

If you are trying to configure your environment in order to maximize the benefits that your home or place of work bestow upon you in terms of health, wealth and relationships, then the Feng Shui Xuan Kong Life Star system is the one for you.

When you combine the two systems and employ them on yourself you will be able to make the most of your best qualities and then seek out an environment which lets you shine and gives the least resistance. A powerful combination of self improvement and informed decision making!

An Easier Life

Life doesn't have to be difficult. It is possible to effectively dodge conflict, problem situations and health problems if you know they are coming. The Life Stars hold the key to many of the "surprises" that life has in store for us and we can learn to shape our environment to our own advantage. This is exciting stuff! Seeking out the best romantic relationships and business opportunities is a top priority for most people and the power of your Life Star can be called upon in these pursuits.

Even though much is made of the layout of the home with relation to Feng Shui, you won't need to bend over backwards to accommodate the advice given in this book. For instance, where you cannot choose the ideal living floor specified, second and third choices are mentioned. You can take as much or as little from this book as you need without fear of it making you paranoid and prey to "paralysis by analysis". Looking back on your own life, you can most probably think of two or three big mistakes – a bad business deal or choice in romantic partner, perhaps. Avoiding pitfalls of this magnitude in the future is made a whole lot easier when you have some idea of how likely they are to occur. If you can make changes to your environment to further reduce this likelihood then all the better!

I hope that this book expands your world view. Once you know how to utilize them, the Nine Stars can be the harbinger of great fortune instead of misery for you. If you can stay on the 'correct side' of your Star and always position yourself to bask in its positive influence then many happy successes await you.

Joey Yap
July, 2011

www.facebook.com/joeyyapFB

Author's personal website :
www.joeyyap.com

Academy websites :
www.masteryacademy.com | www.maelearning.com | www.baziprofiling.com

Three Jade Life Star

Life Star 3	Born in
Male	1925, 1934, 1943, 1952, 1961 1970, 1979, 1988, 1997, 2006
Female	1925, 1934, 1943, 1952, 1961 1970, 1979, 1988, 1997, 2006

- Please note that the date for the Chinese Solar Year starts on Feb 4. This means that if you were born in Feb 2 of 2002, you belong to the previous year 2001.

Your Xuan Kong Life Star

Your Xuan Kong Life Star is Gua #3, and your trigram is called Zhen. It looks like this:

For the rest of this book, we will refer to your Gua #3 as **Life Star 3**.

Basic Attributes of Star 3

Your Life Star 3 is of the (Yang) Wood element and as such, shares some of the traits of Wood. This means that you tend to be somewhat 'wooden' in how you approach things; straight and rigid as opposed to flexible and pliable. On the plus side, this makes you responsible and serious. You play by the rules and tend to enjoy stability.

While you are active and enjoy movement, you dislike being 'uprooted': things have to happen on your terms rather than anyone elses; you prefer certainty over mystery.

As a Star 3 person you tend to have a strong personality and this makes you attractive to others. You command attention when you enter a room. You are helpful and generous to a fault, somewhat like a tree that gives shelter to others but is itself exposed to the elements. Most of the time, it's your second nature to simply look out for others.

Because growth is your main concern, you tend to always think about how you can get to the next stage or level in life and as such are quite frequently impatient and frazzled. You feel an urgent need to get things done and this is because you think everything should have already been done... yesterday! You can be bold and persistent and dogged in going after what you want, and this rouses admiration in others. You are also straightforward and straight-talking because you believe it is the most efficient way to be.

Basic Emotions & Temperament

Plus : Generous, emphatic, flexible, creative, compassion

Minus: Explosive, aggressive, reckless, hasty, prejudice

方向

YOUR FENG SHUI ESSENTIALS

The Feng Shui Essentials comprise Feng Shui Directions, the effects of the Xuan Kong Nine Stars in various sectors and areas of your home and workspace, and the Five Elements.

Each of these factors interact with your Life Star in different ways that will affect how your Life Star manifests itself and determine whether or not it brings out good or bad qualities in you.

Directions

Directions

Direction is an integral component of understanding Xuan Kong Nine Life Stars. Different directions in your home and your place of work can either accentuate or depreciate the strength of your Life Star.

Favorable Direction will highlight or enhance the positive traits of your Life Star, while an Unfavorable Direction will diminish or weaken your Life Star and bring out some of its negative attributes.

The Life Star numbers are categorized into two groups: the East Group and the West Group. The names 'East Group' and 'West Group' are just to demarcate the Greater and Lesser Yin transformation of the Tai Ji. They do not literally represent directions.

East Group Life Stars include 1, 3, 4 and 9. Those who are Life Stars 2, 6, 7 and 8 belong to the West Group. The following table will give you a quick reference of the Auspicious and Inauspicious compass directions of the East and West Group.

East Group 東命

卦 Gua	生氣 Shen Qi Life Generating	天醫 Tian Yi Heavenly Doctor	延年 Yan Nian Longevity	伏位 Fu Wei Stability	禍害 Huo Hai Mishaps	五鬼 Wu Gui Five Ghosts	六煞 Liu Sha Six Killings	絕命 Jue Ming Life Threatening
坎 Kan 1 Water	東南 South East	東 East	南 South	北 North	西 West	東北 North East	西北 North West	西南 South West
震 Zhen 3 Wood	南 South	北 North	東南 South East	東 East	西南 South West	西北 North West	東北 North East	西 West
巽 Xun 4 Wood	北 North	南 South	東 East	東南 South East	西北 North West	西南 South West	西 West	東北 North East
離 Li 9 Fire	東 East	東南 South East	北 North	南 South	東北 North East	西 West	西南 South West	西北 North West

West Group 西命

卦 Gua	生氣 Shen Qi Life Generating	天醫 Tian Yi Heavenly Doctor	延年 Yan Nian Longevity	伏位 Fu Wei Stability	禍害 Huo Hai Mishaps	五鬼 Wu Gui Five Ghosts	六煞 Liu Sha Six Killings	絕命 Jue Ming Life Threatening
坤 Kun 2 Earth	東北 North East	西 West	西北 North West	西南 South West	東 East	東南 South East	南 South	北 North
乾 Qian 6 Metal	西 West	東北 North East	西南 South West	西北 North West	東南 South East	東 East	北 North	南 South
兌 Dui 7 Metal	西北 North West	西南 South West	東北 North East	西 West	北 North	南 South	東南 South East	東 East
艮 Gen 8 Earth	西南 South West	西北 North West	西 West	東北 North East	南 South	北 North	東 East	東南 South East

The concepts of Favorable and Unfavorable are derived from the Eight Wandering Stars system of the Ba Zhai Eight Mansion Feng Shui 八宅風水.

Each of the 8 directions is governed by a Star. These Wandering Stars will affect each Xuan Kong Life Star in different ways. Each Life Star has four Favorable Directions governed by Auspicious Stars: Sheng Qi 生氣 (Life Generating), Tian Yi 天醫 (Heavenly Doctor), Yan Nian 延年 (Longevity), and Fu Wei 伏位 (Stability).

The four Unfavorable Directions are governed by Inauspicious Stars and include Huo Hai 禍害 (Mishaps), Wu Gui 五鬼 (Five Ghost), Liu Sha 六煞 (Six Killings) and Jue Ming 絕命 (Life Diminishing).

The following diagram shows you the Favorable and Unfavorable Directions for Star 3.

Taking the Direction using a Compass

You will need a compass – or alternatively, the Joey Yap iLuoPan app for iPhone available at the Apple App Store – to determine the direction of your Main Door, Bed and Stove. Hold your compass or iLuoPan at waist level as shown on the illustration below. Your compass or iLuoPan will align to the magnetic North on its own. All you need to know is how to take your direction as indicated on the following pages.

Facing Direction of the Main Door

1. Stand about one foot outside the door looking outwards.

2. Use the square base of your compass to help you align yourself parallel to the door.

3. Read the facing direction on your compass.

Facing Direction of the Bed

1. Measure from the head of the bed where your head is placed when you lie down (the direction the headboard faces) and not the direction your feet face.

Facing Direction of the Stove

1. For modern (gas or electric) stoves, look at the where direction of the cooking knobs (fire igniters) are pointing to determine its facing direction.

2. For traditional stoves that require wood and fire to work, look for their 'fire mouth' as the facing direction.

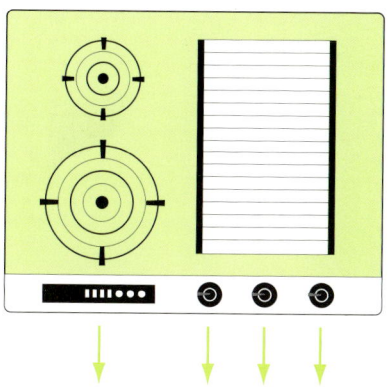

Favorable Directions

South
南 (172.6°-187.5°)

Life Generating
生氣 (Sheng Qi)

The basic characteristics of the Sheng Qi Star:

It brings about promotions, career advancements, strong money and wealth luck, potential political power and authority, and all-round success.

The Sheng Qi Star represents life-generating Qi or energy. It also represents the Wood Element, and hence, governs the facets of success, authority, nobility, status and wealth in life. Wood relates to growth and advancement in life, and as such is an extremely auspicious Star to tap into. For you, the South direction taps into the Sheng Qi potential.

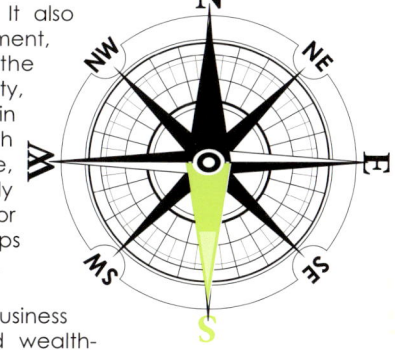

This Star is suitable for business (commercial), career and wealth-related pursuits. It would therefore be ideal for a business or residence to have its Main Door situated in the Sheng Qi sector as it allows you to tap into these energies to create opportunities for profit and long term wealth opportunities.

Sheng Qi is an active star by nature and thus, it is not conducive for rest or sleep-related activities. It is best to avoid having the bed or bedroom located in this sector or for anyone to sleep facing this direction. Use this sector for your work or for active pursuits instead of relaxing ones.

If this sector is missing from a house or is lacking in the office or the premises of a business, the wealth-related aspects of your career or venture will be considerably weakened and it will be a difficult struggle to amass wealth and prosperity.

North
北 (352.6°-7.5°)

Heavenly Doctor
天醫 *(Tian Yi)*

The basic characteristics of the Tian Yi Star:

It brings about general good luck and well-being, as well as positive mentor luck or the presence of sound advisors and guidance.

This Star represents the Earth Element and is therefore the determinant of noble people (mentors) and people of caliber and status. It also denotes your health prospects and physical wellbeing. As such, the Tian Yi Star is best utilized to help generate guidance for your career or for any project which you've embarked upon. It will bring about the help and assistance of others.

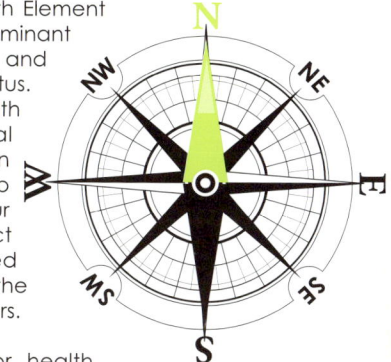

It is also a useful Star for health purposes, and its benefits can be employed when you need to recuperate, recover, or heal from an illness, surgical procedure or health issue.

When the Tian Yin sector is missing from a home or office, your health is likely to suffer because of it. In addition, you will also find help from noble people hard to come by, especially in times of need in life and career matters. You will come across more obstacles and obstructions which you must overcome on your own without the external help of others.

Since the Tian Yi Star represents nobility, it also governs your reputation, respectability, and your oratory powers. It thus has influence on your powers of speech and persuasion, and has some bearing on how you are perceived by others and how well they respond to your verbal overtures.

Southeast
東南 (127.6°-142.5°)

Longevity
延年 (Yan Nian)

The basic characteristics of the Yan Nian Star:

It prolongs and enhances life and improves the quality of your life. It promotes good communication with others which in turn makes for good relationships.

The Yan Nian Star represents the Metal Element, and as such governs speech and the effectiveness of your words. If you are looking to establish good relationships and rapport with others, you will need the help of this Star, since it governs aspects of successful networking, communication and relationship building.

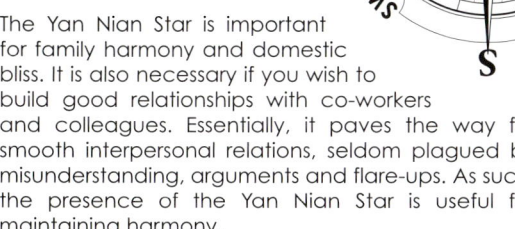

The Yan Nian Star is important for family harmony and domestic bliss. It is also necessary if you wish to build good relationships with co-workers and colleagues. Essentially, it paves the way for smooth interpersonal relations, seldom plagued by misunderstanding, arguments and flare-ups. As such, the presence of the Yan Nian Star is useful for maintaining harmony.

If you are employed in public relations or marketing and you must interact with clients and customers as part of your daily routine, you will find the Qi brought about by this Star very useful to your career.

Do note that if the Yan Nian sector is missing, harmony and unity will be adversely affected, and relations are likely to be tense or strained. At the very least, you can expect more argument and discord with others.

East
東 (82.6°-97.5°)

Stability
伏位 *(Fu Wei)*

The basic characteristics of the Fu Wei Star:

It is a Star that promotes calm and keeps you grounded. It allows for peace of mind and rationality. It also promotes good luck.

The Fu Wei Star represents the Wood Element. When qualities or virtues such as calmness and tranquility are required, this is the Star you need! It promotes peace of mind and heightens clarity of thought, so this is also the Star to use if you need to focus, study or make important decisions.

If you wish to practice mediation or undertake religious and spiritual observances, the Fu Wei Star will provide the energies needed for calm and serenity, enhancing mental health and wellbeing.

This Star is most suitably applied to libraries, study areas/zones or other places where concentration is necessary. When considering the home or workplace, this Star can help create areas where the mind can be easily quietened and people can reflect and turn inward.

When the Fu Wei sector is missing from a place, peace of mind will be difficult to attain.

Unfavorable Directions

Southwest
西南 (217.6°-232.5°)

Mishaps
祸害 (Huo Hai)

The basic characteristics of the Huo Hai Star: It denotes potential calamities, accidents, and mishaps. It undermines good efforts and brings about the risk of mistakes and errors.

The Huo Hai Star represents the Earth Element and is the harbinger of mishaps, loss of wealth, sudden (unfortunate) changes or hassles as well as work-related obstacles. What it does is undermine your efforts and bring about sudden obstructions or problems that will result in a loss of time and energy.

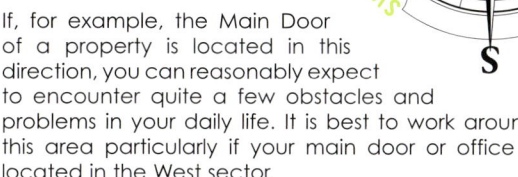

If, for example, the Main Door of a property is located in this direction, you can reasonably expect to encounter quite a few obstacles and problems in your daily life. It is best to work around this area particularly if your main door or office is located in the West sector.

The detrimental effects of a negative star are compounded when it is located within an area that is already affected by negative Feng Shui, so pay attention to the negative structures outside this area.

Northwest
西北 (307.6°-322.5°)

Five Ghosts
五鬼 (Wu Gui)

The basic characteristics of the Wu Gui Star:

It brings about betrayal and treachery through back-stabbing, gossip, and rumors. It also denotes endless bickering and fraught tension brought about by arguments.

The Wu Gui Star represents the Fire Element and is the bringer of betrayal, ill-intentioned gossip, rumours, backstabbing, cruelty, petty people and even subterfuge and sabotage. It generally denotes a sense of unease brought upon by less-than-honest speech.

The presence of Wu Gui in a house causes disloyalty and discord amongst family members, affecting relationships and marriages. If it is present in your work place, then you should also watch out for fights and arguments between your colleagues or subordinates and friction or tension with your superiors.

Negative external forms such as (sharp) pylons and jagged rooftops pointing towards a house further aggravate the effects of this Star.

Northeast
東北 (37.6°-52.5°)

Six Killings
六煞 *(Liu Sha)*

The basic characteristics of the Liu Sha Star:

This Star brings about injuries and accidents. It also denotes the possibility of betrayals and dishonesty, and the risk of potential scandals.

The Liu Sha Star relates to the element of Water and is the harbinger of lawsuits and potential scandals. Legal problems at the workplace or adulterous affairs in relation to your marriage or personal relationships could be brought to light.

This Star is also the harbinger of bodily injury, harm and conditions requiring people to undergo physical surgery. Robberies and theft are also likely, and you will have to be careful about what information you share with others and with the general safety of your personal documents and possessions.

Be mindful of the presence of negative external forms, which will compound the adverse effects of this Star. For instance, a Y-shaped road at the Liu Sha sector will result in scandalous affairs, while negative structures as mentioned earlier will compound and exacerbate the harmful effects of the Liu Sha Star.

West
西 (262.6°-277.5°)

Life Threatening
絕命 (Jue Ming)

The basic characteristics of the Jue Ming Star:

It brings about the risk of accidents and major illness, and the threat of miscarriage for pregnant women. It also signals potential for great calamity.

This Star represents the Metal Element and it signifies accidents and illnesses. The energies of the Jue Ming Star are quite severe and so are its adverse effects, bringing with it considerable risk.

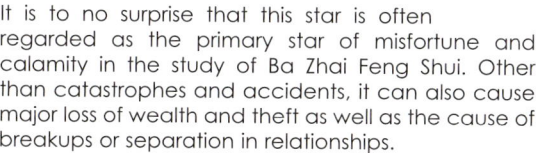

In severe cases, the Jue Ming Star can even cause fatal accidents, ailments or injuries when there are negative external forms outside of the West sector.

It is to no surprise that this star is often regarded as the primary star of misfortune and calamity in the study of Ba Zhai Feng Shui. Other than catastrophes and accidents, it can also cause major loss of wealth and theft as well as the cause of breakups or separation in relationships.

Bed Alignment Direction

One of the key Feng Shui factors of the bedroom is how your bed is placed. For starters, your bed should preferably be pushed against a wall, with the headboard also against it. The most important thing you can do when laying out your bedroom with regards to Feng Shui is to make sure your headboard is aligned with your Favorable Direction.

Facing Direction, in the case of bed alignment, refers to the direction of your headboard. This means it is the direction your head faces when you lie down on the bed, and **not** the direction that your feet face.

As a Star 3, your Bed Alignment Directions are:

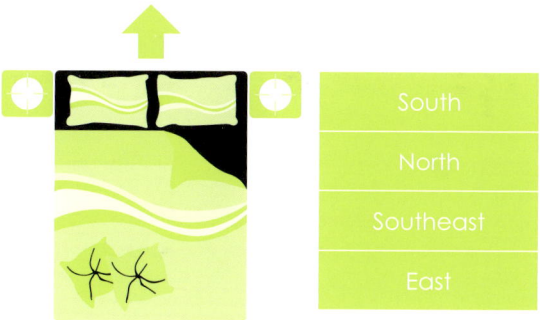

- South
- North
- Southeast
- East

Best Floor

A reality of modern life is that most of us do not live in houses these days, instead living in multi story apartments and condominium blocks.

Some of us are pretty mobile and live a nomad-like lifestyle that may require us to stay in high-rise buildings for certain periods of time. As such, it becomes important to select the right floor to reside in. The objective of this is to achieve elemental affinity between you (the occupant) with the energies of a particular floor.

As you are a Star 3 person of the Wood element, the chart below gives you the best floors for you to live on in terms of first choice, second choice, and third choice.

First Choice	Second Choice	Third Choice
3rd Floor	1st Floor	2nd Floor
8th Floor	6th Floor	7th Floor
13th Floor	11th Floor	12th Floor
18th Floor	16th Floor	17th Floor
23th Floor	21th Floor	22th Floor
28th Floor	26th Floor	27th Floor
33th Floor	31th Floor	32th Floor
38th Floor	36th Floor	37th Floor
43st Floor	41st Floor	42th Floor
48th Floor	46th Floor	47th Floor

Select :
Water Shaped buildings & Wood Shaped buildings

Avoid :
Metal shaped buildings and Fire shaped buildings

Personal Grand Duke Directions

Identifying the Grand Duke Sector is important. Your Personal Grand Duke Sector relates to your birth year. For example, if you are born in the year of the Rat then the Rat is your Personal Grand Duke and we know that the Rat sector is North 2.

We want to avoid the harmful properties of this area and as you are a Star 3 person, you can locate your Personal Grand Duke Sector in the following directions:

Personal Grand Duke Directions for Male

MALE Birth Year	Personal Grand Duke	Direction
1916, 1952, 1988, 2024	辰 Chen Dragon	東南 1 Southeast 1
1925, 1961, 1997, 2033	丑 Chou Ox	東北 1 Northeast 1
1934, 1970, 2006, 2042	戌 Xu Dog	西北 1 Northwest 1
1943, 1979, 2015, 2051	未 Wei Goat	西南 1 Southwest 1

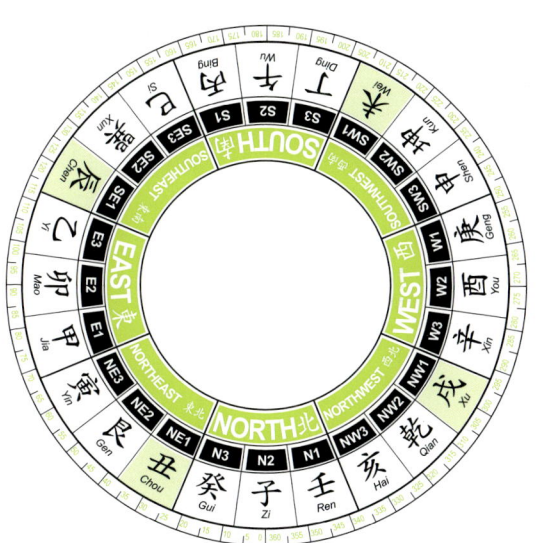

Personal Grand Duke Directions for Female

FEMALE Birth Year	Personal Grand Duke	Direction
1916, 1952, 1988, 2024	辰 Chen Dragon	東南 1 Southeast 1
1925, 1961, 1997, 2033	丑 Chou Ox	東北 1 Northeast 1
1934, 1970, 2006, 2042	戌 Xu Dog	西北 1 Northwest 1
1943, 1979, 2015, 2051	未 Wei Goat	西南 1 Southwest 1

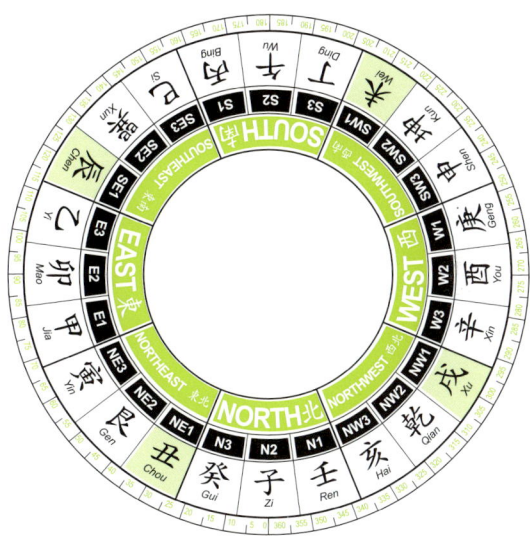

Ideally, you should not have a bathroom or toilet located in these areas of your home above and Sha Qi external features such as pylons, T-junctions, Dead Tree should be avoided. The Sha Qi in the Personal Grand Duke Sector is extremely strong and so all efforts to avoid spending a lot of time in it should be made. It goes without saying that the Personal Grand Duke Sector of your home is not the ideal spot for a bedroom! The Sha Qi in this area of the home is so strong in fact that it is difficult for any further negative Qi to enter!

Personal Clash Directions

Your home will contain Personal Clash Sectors. Spending time in these areas of your home will bring up problems in your life with significant others. As a Star 3 person, you will find your Personal Clash Sectors in the following directions:

Personal Clash Directions for Male

MALE Birth Year	Personal Clash Sector	Direction
1916, 1952, 1988, 2024	戌 Xu Dog	西北1 Northwest 1
1925, 1961, 1997, 2033	未 Wei Goat	西南1 Southwest 1
1934, 1970, 2006, 2042	辰 Chen Dragon	東南1 Southeast 1
1943, 1979, 2015, 2051	丑 Chou Ox	東北1 Northeast 1

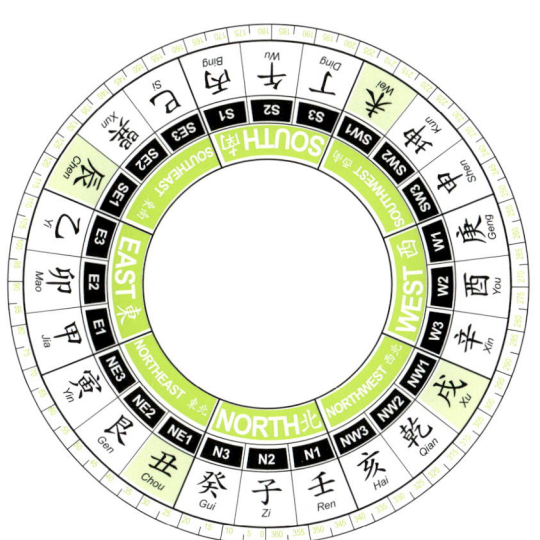

Personal Clash Directions for Female

FEMALE Birth Year	Personal Grand Duke	Direction
1916, 1952, 1988, 2024	戌 Xu Dog	西北 1 Northwest 1
1925, 1961, 1997, 2033	未 Wei Goat	西南 1 Southwest 1
1934, 1970, 2006, 2042	辰 Chen Dragon	東南 1 Southeast 1
1943, 1979, 2015, 2051	丑 Chou Ox	東北 1 Northeast 1

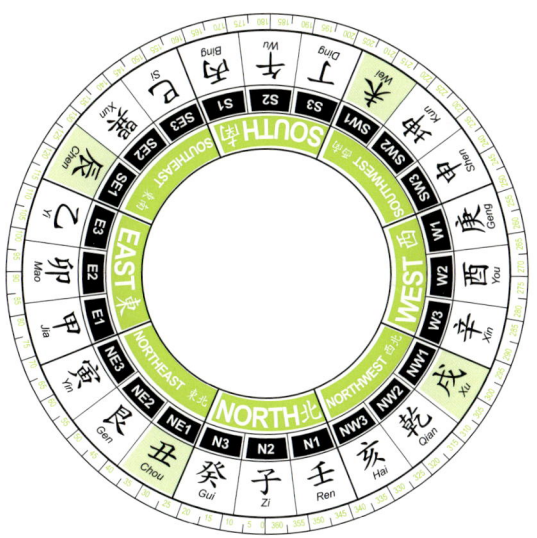

The locations above are a bad place for important features of your home such as the main door, bedroom and kitchen. You should seek to avoid these sectors in the same way you avoid your Personal Grand Duke Sector.

Flying Stars Effects

Each year, the Xuan Kong Flying Stars fly into a different section of a property, be it your residence or your work space. The effects that these Nine Stars have on you will be different depending on your Life Star. In this section you can find out how different Flying Stars in different sectors will effect you with regards to Feng Shui.

The Flying Stars have both negative and positive attributes, but which facets will show when you see a particular Star, depends on the timeliness and the period.

A few of the Nine Stars are inherently negative, a few are inherently positive in nature and some can be both good and bad. Even then, we must remember that the Stars have the capacity to manifest either their positive or negative facets because in Feng Shui, nothing is ever inherently bad or good forever.

When it comes to Flying Stars, it is important to remember this key principle: Forms activate the Stars and the Stars in turn influence the People. This is what you should keep in mind as you read about the effects of the Nine Stars on your Life Star.

1 ★ → 3 Jade Life

The effects of the visiting #1 White Star on a 3 Jade Life:

In terms of Feng Shui effects, the presence of the #1 White Star on a Star 3 person can bring about quite a few disputes and arguments. These fights can be quite bitter, and if left to worsen, can eventually spiral into lawsuits. Bear this in mind, in particular, at the workplace. Stay out of arguments if you can and do not say rash things in the heat of the moment which could incriminate you later on. The likelihood of robbery, theft, and potential financial loss is increased by this #1 White. This is due to the interference of some unscrupulous third parties or external factors so keep your guard up. Health problems are also made more likely, with liver issues and dizzy spells being occurring. If the #1 White is in your bedroom, it will help with your learning/intelligence but may increase your levels of aggression or disposition towards violence.

2★ → 3 Jade Life

The effects of the visiting #2 Black Star on a 3 Jade Life:

In terms of Feng Shui effects, the presence of the #2 Black results in Bullfight Sha, which means essentially a clash of wills and words. As such, arguments and disputes will be prevalent. You will find yourself at a crossroads with others, engaging in frequent verbal spats. This is particularly true for mothers and sons living in the same house. Furthermore, the presence of #2 Black brings with it some health consequences to deal with. This is likely to be in the form of stomach illnesses and digestive problems. In general, the #2 Black also brings about food and nutrition-related issues, so you must pay more attention to your dietary habits and food intake.

3★ → 3 Jade Life

The effects of the visiting **#3 Jade Star** on a **3 Jade Life:**

In terms of Feng Shui effects, Star 3 people under the influence of the #3 Jade Star are likely to be a little cold in their interactions with others for a time period. They will find it harder to emphathise with others or make an attempt to reach out. This could lead to some intense arguments, or worse, lead to the erosion or worsening of valuable ties. Another effect of the presence of the #3 Jade is emotional turbulence, which could lead to some extreme forms of thought. Hysteria is possible, and will be exacerbated if your nerves are already fraught.

4★ → 3 Jade Life

The effects of the visiting #4 Green Star on a 3 Jade Life:

In terms of Feng Shui effects, the presence of the #4 Green is likely to help men of the Life Star 3, as you will find it boosting your love life! If you're single and looking for romantic prospects, the presence of the #4 Green will help speed things along. Therefore, you will find yourself with the opportunity to meet new people even when you least expect it. However, if there are negative structures outside the sector with the #4 Green, then some form of violence or aggression is likely to afflict you. At the same time, you will have to guard against financial fraud and embezzlement. Pay more attention to the state of your finances, particularly if you run a business or are in a partnership.

5★ → 3 Jade Life

The effects of the visiting **#5 Yellow Star** on a **3 Jade Life**:

In terms of Feng Shui effects, the presence of the #5 Yellow can result in a loss of fortune. This is particularly true if you're someone who likes to take a gamble with your finances. As such, your natural inclination to go for risky investments should be curtailed with the presence of the #5 Yellow, as the outcome could be disastrous.

The #5 Yellow is also bad for your health, and could lead to some problems with your liver and an increased chance of infectious illness. Furthermore, you will have to be cautious with your physical health during your day to day activities, as accidents and injuries are likely to be a significant risk. Broken limbs may also be a possibility.

6★ → 3 Jade Life

The effects of the visiting #6 White Star on a 3 Jade Life:

In terms of Feng Shui effects, the presence of the #6 White is likely to have some negative effects on your health, primarily. Headaches, migraine and a lack of energy brought about by physical problems will also lead you to feel listless and uninspired.

Injuries are also possible, especially accidental ones brought about by the use of sharp metal implements. Be careful when you do any cutting, slicing, and dicing in and around the home or at work, particularly if you work with dangerous tools.

7★ → 3 Jade Life

The effects of the visiting #7 Red Star on a 3 Jade Life:

In terms of Feng Shui effects, the presence of the #7 Red doesn't bode too well for you, especially where your finances are concerned. The outcome is likely to be one of significant loss in your finances. This will probably be due to robbery and theft, so you need to be more careful. Loss of finance is also likely to happen through fraud, so pay attention to the financial goings-on around particularly if you're in business. Observe the state of your investments closely. There is also the chance that in some dire situations, you end up losing money through lawsuits. In fact, #7 Red also brings about betrayal or treachery by a friend or family member that could result in this lawsuit.

8★ → 3 Jade Life

The effects of the visiting #8 White Star on a 3 Jade Life:

In terms of Feng Shui effects, the presence of the #8 White may be detrimental to young men of Life Star 3. Health issues are likely to be quite serious in the form of asthma or respiratory disease. Some form of ailment or problems involving the heart are also a possible risk. Furthermore, pregnant Star 3 women need to be aware of the increased potential for complications. The #8 White is also a risk for familial relations, bringing with it an abundance of trouble and strife, increasing the risk of divorces or separation. However, if the positive effects are enhanced through Feng Shui remedies, then the #8 White can bring about good financial prospects.

9★ → 3 Jade Life

The effects of the visiting **#9 Purple Star** on a **3 Jade Life:**

In terms of Feng Shui effects, this can be very good for the Star 3 person's mental and creative developments. When the positive aspects of the #9 Purple are enhanced, you will enjoy clarity of thought and an improvement in all work that requires your imagination, intelligence, and creativity. For your career, it could well mean a professional advancement or potential promotion. However, if there are negative structures outside the sector of #9 Purple, then there could be risks of a fire-hazard or some form of danger involving fire, including electrical components and wiring.

THE FIVE ELEMENTS

The Five Elements

The element of your Life Star 3 is (Yang) Wood, and it is important that you understand the implications of this. In the study of Chinese Metaphysics and Feng Shui, a basic understanding of the Five Elements is integral to success. This section will briefly outline the role of the Five Elements.

The Five Elements are symbolic representations of energy, or Qi. In Feng Shui and in BaZi, the Five Elements are Earth, Metal, Water, Wood, and Fire. Wood represents benevolence and growth. Wood is straight and set in its way, but with a tendency to reach for the top – like a tree that grows. To visualise Wood, think of something long and flat, like a log. The colour usually associated with this is dark green.

In order to understand the elements, it's important to understand their relationship to one another. Each element does not exist in isolation. As such, these elements share three important relationships known as 'cycles' that are fundamental to the understanding of Feng Shui: the Productive Cycle, the Controlling Cycle, and the Weakening Cycle.

Productive Cycle

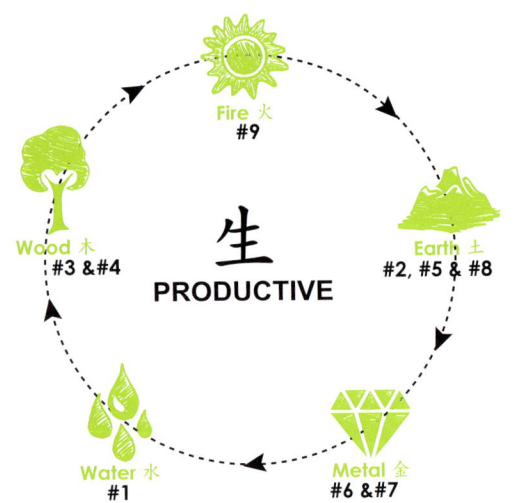

In this cycle,

| Water produces Wood |
| Wood produces Fire |
| Fire produces Earth |
| Earth produces Metal |
| Metal produces Water |

This is a cycle where the elements "produce" one another in terms of providing or helping the growth of another. In the case of Water, then, it produces nourishment for trees and plants (i.e. Wood). An element that produces another element means that it strengthens and grows the element that it produces. Here are some simple metaphors might help you visualize this better:

Water waters soil, producing Wood
Wood makes kindling, producing Fire
Fire makes ashes, producing Earth
Earth is mined, producing Metal
Metal melts, producing Water

Controlling Cycle

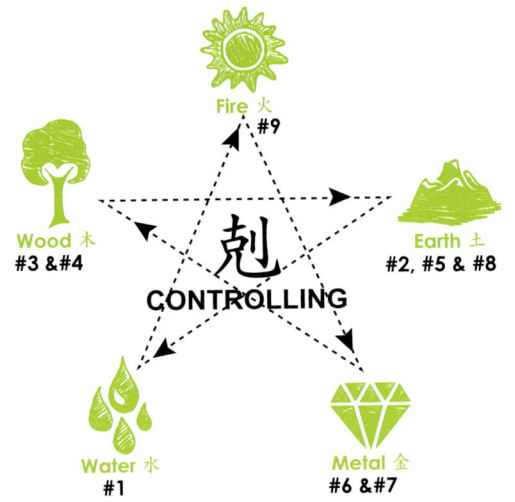

In this cycle,

| Fire controls Metal |
| Metal controls Wood |
| Wood controls Earth |
| Earth controls Water |
| Water controls Fire |

This is a cycle where the elements keep each under in "control": an element is countered or subjugated by its controlling element. In this instance, for example, the element of Water controls Fire by putting it out. Here are some simple metaphors to help you visualize it better:

Water extinguishes Fire
Fire melts Metal
Metal cuts Wood
Wood roots tightly grip Earth
Earth contains Water

Weakening Cycle

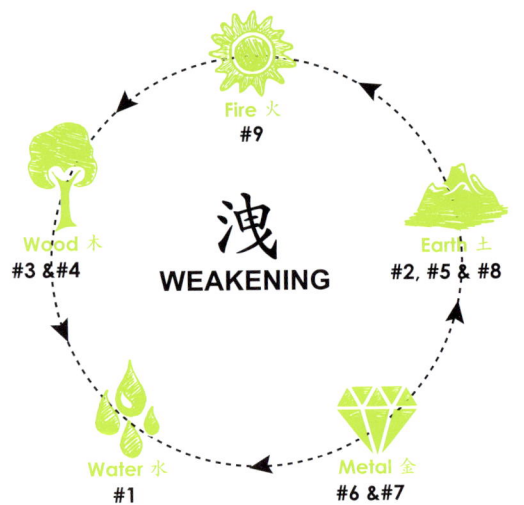

In this cycle,

| Water weakens Metal |
| Metal weakens Earth |
| Earth weakens Fire |
| Fire weakens Wood |
| Wood weakens Water |

The Weakening Cycle can be best understood as the reverse of the Productive Cycle, in that the strength of the element is weakened by another in order to keep it in check. Remember, the key to Qi in Feng Shui is balance, and different elements keep other elements from becoming too strong. For example, Wood absorbs Water and therefore weakens it. Again, here are some metaphors for easier visualization:

Water can be partly absorbed by Wood
Wood can be partly burnt by Fire
Fire can be diminished with Earth
Earth is weakened when mined for Metal
Metal is corroded by Water

The following table shows you the Annual Stars for the year 2000 to 2026.

Examine it and figure out where your room lies; in which sector. Take note of the element of that sector and remember that as a Star 3 person, your element is Wood.

SE	S	SW
6 White METAL	2 Black EARTH	4 Green WOOD
5 Yellow EARTH	7 Red METAL	9 Purple FIRE
1 White WATER	3 Jade WOOD	8 White EARTH

2002, 2011, 2020

SE	S	SW
5 Yellow EARTH	1 White WATER	3 Jade WOOD
4 Green WOOD	6 White METAL	8 White EARTH
9 Purple FIRE	2 Black EARTH	7 Red METAL

2003, 2012, 2021

SE	S	SW
4 Green WOOD	9 Purple FIRE	2 Black EARTH
3 Jade WOOD	5 Yellow EARTH	7 Red METAL
8 White EARTH	1 White WATER	6 White METAL

2004, 2013, 2022

SE	S	SW
3 Jade WOOD	8 White EARTH	1 White WATER
2 Black EARTH	4 Green WOOD	6 White METAL
7 Red METAL	9 Purple FIRE	5 Yellow EARTH

2005, 2014, 2023

SE	S	SW
2 Black EARTH	7 Red METAL	9 Purple FIRE
1 White WATER	3 Jade WOOD	5 Yellow EARTH
6 White METAL	8 White EARTH	4 Green WOOD

2006, 2015, 2024

SE	S	SW
1 White WATER	6 White METAL	8 White EARTH
9 Purple FIRE	2 Black EARTH	4 Green WOOD
5 Yellow EARTH	7 Red METAL	3 Jade WOOD

2007, 2016, 2025

SE	S	SW
9 Purple FIRE	5 Yellow EARTH	7 Red METAL
8 White EARTH	1 White WATER	3 Jade WOOD
4 Green WOOD	6 White METAL	2 Black EARTH

2008, 2017, 2026

SE	S	SW
8 White EARTH	4 Green WOOD	6 White METAL
7 Red METAL	9 Purple FIRE	2 Black EARTH
3 Jade WOOD	5 Yellow EARTH	1 White WATER

2000, 2009, 2018

SE	S	SW
7 Red METAL	3 Jade WOOD	5 Yellow EARTH
6 White METAL	8 White EARTH	1 White WATER
2 Black EARTH	4 Green WOOD	9 Purple FIRE

2001, 2010, 2019

These Annual Stars shows you the location of the Stars in a property for the duration of the years specified. Based on the year, the Annual Stars will be located in different sectors of the house. Accordingly, different Annual Stars will affect the Feng Shui of your room in different years.

If the Annual Star of your bedroom is of the same element as your Life Star then the outcome is likely to be prosperous (Productive Cycle). If the Annual Star is your Life Star's controlling element (Controlling Cycle), then the result is likely to be stressful – although this combination is still desirable. But if the Annual Star element is the countering element (Countering Cycle) of your Life Star, then the combination is an unfavorable or inauspicious one for you. (Special note: the #5 Yellow Star is generally an undesirable Annual Star for your bedroom regardless of your Life Star.)

Think about the way the element of the Annual Star and your element (Wood) interact.

Besides the Annual Stars of the year, there also other factors to be considered. These include the Flying Stars chart of your specific house or property with the Sitting and Facing Stars. Advanced students may want to read *Xuan Kong Flying Stars Feng Shui* for further information. These Stars also affect the evaluation of the impact of the Xuan Kong Flying Stars on your property. There are many other ways of assessing the Feng Shui of a property, and it's important to understand that all these factors play an important and related role.

Characteristics of Star 3

We all have our "good days" and "bad days". Feng Shui seeks to help isolate why this happens and provide advice that you can use to make every day a "good day" where you are in your element. This section outlines the good and bad characteristics of your Life Star. In a positive sector of your house or work, the positive attributes of your Life Star will be further enhanced, and you will display more of these characteristics. In a negative sector, the positive attributes will be diminished and the negative attributes will begin to show through. Your bad characteristics will take center stage.

The Good

Persevering

As a Star 3 person, you possess the qualities of Yang Wood which makes you unstoppable. In this sense, you are almost like a tree that does not quit growing halfway – it only stops when it is done. As such, you also possess a sort of can-do attitude and energy that gives you the momentum to stay on a project or a particular course until you get what you want.

Bold

You have courage in spades and you are not afraid to use it. As such, you tend to be someone who fuses both a sense of perseverance with boldness in order to get what you want. You're not easily cowed by threats or obstructions. Your strong personality provides a buffer from the world, and you can therefore be described as 'thick-skinned' in that things don't easily break or offend you.

Frank

One of your most distinctive characteristics as a Star 3 person is your ability to be absolutely straightforward and frank. Honesty is a hallmark of Star 3 people and you speak plainly and dislike obfuscation or sophisticated talk. Pretty words and fulsome language only makes you impatient and irritated! As such, you usually find yourself incapable of false small talk or flattery, and tend to speak your mind without fear or embarrassment.

Active

Despite your comfort with stability and your somewhat calm external appearance, you tend to have quite a bit of liveliness in you. You feel the need to keep moving. This can be seen in a more day-to-day sense, where you dislike having to stay in one place for too long. As such, you tend to gravitate towards jobs that utilize your lively energy.

壞

The Bad

Stubborn

Because you tend to have your mind set on things, you can become quite rigid and unyielding when you focus on something for too long. You tend to be inflexible and want things to go only in the way you prescribe. Also, if you want something, then you expect to get it immediately. You lack the ability to understand the reasons that lie behind a delay or a change, and this can make you unreasonable.

Rash

"Fools rush in where angels fear to tread" is a popular saying, and sometimes this explains the Star 3 character when it's unhealthy! Because of your dislike for waiting and your zeal to get ahead, you can be rash and unthinking, rushing into something before you've even considered the outcome. You tend to disregard the importance of measured thought and patience before taking action, often overemphasizing the value of the action itself.

Blunt

If there's one thing you're not, it's diplomatic! When delivered in the right way at the right time, honesty is a wonderfully refreshing trait. Sometimes people appreciate that your unique ability to tell it as it is. However, there is a fine line between honest and rude, and sometimes you may find it hard to tell the difference. You often run off your mouth and may say things that aggravate or upset others because so long as it's true you feel it needs to be said. You may lack the sensitivity that will help you choose the right words when you need to be subtle, because honesty doesn't always work all the time.

Temperamental

You can be somewhat chaotic in your approach to matters and you are a slave to your changing emotions. As such, when in an unhealthy state of mind, you can be a temperamental person who finds it hard to get your feelings in order. Others may find it difficult to orientate themselves to your particular frame of mind, depending on what you're doing or thinking. This lack of structure can create a sense of disturbance and confusion.

職業和財富

CAREER AND WEALTH

Characteristics at Work

As a Star 3 person, you may display some of these basic characteristics in professional situations at the workplace and in relation to your career. Being aware of your own key characteristics will help you understand why you act and react to situations, people, and tasks in the way you do.

This section outlines the good and bad characteristics of your Life Star. In a positive sector of your house or work, the positive attributes of your Life Star will be further enhanced, and you will display more of these characteristics. In a negative sector, the positive attributes will be diminished and the negative attributes will begin to show through. Your bad characteristics will take center stage.

- ## Outgoing

Where your day-to-day work tasks are concerned, you prefer a role that allows you to engage with other people and take a more hands-on role with social networking and connections. You are not quite comfortable in a passive or behind-the-scenes job role, as this will make you feel restless and less inclined to give it your all. You like being where the action is, and quiet, unobtrusive roles don't suit you.

- ## Inspired

Once you find something that interests you, you can become extremely active and committed to finishing it. As a Star 3 person, motivation is one of your intrinsic qualities and you are proud of this. It is what gives you the drive to do more or create something better. At work, others view you as a valuable player precisely because of this sense of inspiration.

- ## Aggressive

Most Star 3 people tend to achieve success and wealth at a young age, largely due to their never-say-die attitude. You are aggressive in fulfilling your goals and often move up the career ladder quickly. You are good at convincing and persuading clients and/or customers to take action, making you good at your job.

- ## Confident

One of the key characteristics of a Star 3 person at work is the ability to plough ahead without overwhelming moments of self-doubt or deprecation. In a word, you can be very confident and blaze a trail of certainty – that is, if you're working on something that plays to your natural strengths. As such, colleagues and subordinates may tend to look up to you or naturally expect you to lead.

Suitable Job Roles

• Communications, public relations, tourism

These are all job roles that will enable you to enjoy a variety of experiences and situations, and this is something that will give you the energy and inspiration to work harder. As you enjoy meeting people and persuading them and winning them over, anything that puts you in social situations where you can do this will play to your inherent strengths.

- ## Politician (or in politics)

You engage well with people, and your drive for ambition and keen interest in winning means that you will have the strength and dedication to persevere through the often arduous climb to the top. You also have the aggressive, thick-skinned nature that is essential for ensuring that you do not become easily offended or disheartened in what is often a ruthless rat-race.

- ## Journalist

You have the right qualities to make a good journalist, particularly a broadcast journalist or an investigative reporter. You will not back down from a story, and will push forward aggressively until you get what you need. Furthermore,

you're not self-conscious or shy and are not hampered by too many "what-ifs", and will thus find that you don't back down when you need to work hard to get a quote or an interview.

• Broadcaster, emcee, TV anchor/presenter

As a Star 3 personality that is confident and outgoing, you do enjoy being under the spotlight and may even thrive while you're under it! Furthermore, a busy schedule that keeps you moving is exactly the kind of thing you enjoy. You tend to enjoy talking, as well, and like to keep others entertained by a creative use of actions and words.

Career and Wealth Guide

• Temper your words

As a Star 3 person, one of your best and worst traits is your tendency to speak plainly and at times, rather bluntly. However, in terms of moving up the career ladder or getting people to like you (an essential part of networking!) it is fairly crucial to know how to say the right things at the right time. In addition to knowing how to woo people with the right words, learning to be diplomatic will help to avoid needless arguments, tension, and misunderstanding.

- ## Cultivate patience

It is true that good things come to those who wait, and this applies both in your personal life and in matters of career and wealth. Being impatient means that you sometimes lack the foresight to implement potentially beneficial long-term plans which require you to hunker down for the long-haul. Similarly, being impatient with money means that you always go for the short-term, rapid fire investment – and miss out on some protracted investments that could yield good returns throughout your life.

- ## Cultivate leadership

    Ideally, you wish to be in a situation where everyone wins. As such, you make a good leader because you will strive to create an environment that benefits each member of your team or department. However, you will have to ensure that others see you as leadership-material – and this means proving to them that you can be stable, reliable, and trustworthy and not just a ball of intense energy!

- ## Moderation in wealth pursuit

Your appetite for more certainly serves you well, but in terms of finance you need to understand that there are prosperous periods of time and there are less prosperous periods of time. Guard against unvarnished insatiability that prompts you to think of more money even in times when you should scale back and save. Live modestly, and avoid splurging – it's one of your biggest weaknesses.

• Learn to organize

Your rushed and hurried manner may get you through a lot of events without scrapes, but to make strides in your career it will certainly help to have a plan. A back-up plan may be the thing that allows you to get away with taking risks and rushing into big projects. Being consistently proactive with a schedule to keep you in line will also help your colleagues and superiors take you seriously.

Famous Personalities:

Margaret Thatcher, Barrack Obama, Princess Diana of Wales, George Clooney

人際關係

RELATIONSHIPS

Guide for Relationships

As a Star 3 person, you approach love and relationships in the same way you approach everything else – with gusto. You love hard, and tend to show it. You can be extremely passionate, and you don't give up easily. If you've set your sights on someone, you are likely to do everything in your power to please and win over him or her.

This is a good thing, until it's not! That is, you need to guard against being aggressive. Being forceful and aggressive may work for you in your job, for example, if you are in a line of work that requires you to pursue, persuade, and win over people for sales and profit. But in matters of the heart, your approach should be softer, or you risk turning people or scaring them off! For this reason, you need to understand what the other party is feeling, and how they respond. If they back away, don't intensify your efforts. Instead, play it cool and give them space – love, after all, is an intricate dance!

You may have problems sustaining interest in a relationship because you fall head over heels at the start but then find yourself becoming bored in the long run. For that reason, don't focus on infatuation. Be more circumspect with the people you choose to date or ask out. Once you meet someone who is right for you, you're actually the "marrying type." You settle down well and enjoy comfort and stability at home. You will enjoy a good family life that is peaceful and harmonious. Until then, take your time in meeting someone who is right for you. Don't rush things if it doesn't feel right.

Finally, it will be important for you to learn how to navigate arguments. It's not always the case that you have to be blatantly honest with your partner. This is not to say that you have to take refuge in lies, rather, you will have to learn when it is the right time to say something, and the right time to hold your tongue. Inevitably, all that is important will have to be spoken of plainly and honestly at some point in the future, but to make a relationship work you have to learn to be kind with your words so that you don't hurt your partner. Although your intentions are rarely bad, the other party will have a difficult time knowing this.

Star 3 in relationships:

Star 3 people are often overly possessive and experience jealousy. They need to work on their romantic and emotional natures.

HEALTH

Guide for Health

Body parts and organs that are related to Star 3: Liver and gallbladder.

Your Star 3 represents the liver and gallbladder, and also the veins, to a lesser extent. As such, you need to be on the lookout for potential liver problems or diseases that could crop up. Part of your susceptibility lies in your lifestyle – you dislike saying no to pleasure and love to overindulge, be it in food or wine! Spending too much having a good time socially is bad enough but when you also then proceed to throwing yourself into your work all the time, you may not have enough time to exercise. This can can exacerbate the health problems you're likely to have. Guard against over-consumption of alcohol at all times.

In terms of your veins and nerves, you are likely to have weakness or pain, particularly around your neck. Try to avoid muscle sprains which tend to come easily for you. Frequent exercise, particularly the kind that incorporates pilates or yoga, will help make you more flexible and supple and assist in relaxing your muscles. Your nervous system may also be a sensitive one. Part of the blame for this can be placed at your own feet because your lifestyle leaves you prey to stress and nervous tension.

When you do become ill, you tend to become very ill. Your lungs and breathing system tend to be affected the most. As such, be careful when you contract coughs, tonsillitis, or any form of respiratory disease. It will be best to allow yourself to fully recover and to seek proper treatment, instead of ignoring the problem. Ensure you get enough rest and don't constantly push yourself beyond the brink for the purpose of keeping up with work and social engagements.

Potential health concerns:

Gallbladder stones & infection

Heat-related problems, including 'heatiness'

Fever

Sprains and fractures

Injuries arising

COMPATIBILITY WITH OTHER LIFE STARS

This section examines your compatibility as a Star 3 with other people who have the same and different Stars. No person goes through life completely alone. Relationships with others form the bedrock of good career networking. Friendships and relations with loved ones, spouses, partners and family make everything worth while. It is necessary to understand how compatible people with different Stars are to prevent conflict and missed opportunities. Bear in mind that issues of compatibility are not definite or set in stone. There are exceptions to every rule. In addition, **the quality of Feng Shui** in your environment helps dictate whether positive or negative traits in people manifest themselves and thus it weighs in on the quality of your relationships with those people. This section serves as a good guide on your relationships with other people of different Stars.

At a glance, Star 3 people are generally quite popular among others and tend to typically enjoy good relations with the people in their life. You will generally have safe relationships with Stars 1, 3, 4, 2, 5, and 8. But you will have to be cautious with people who are of Star 6, 7, and 9.

You will enjoy a good relationship with Star 4 people because your personalities will be similar, and there will be plenty of mutual help and assistance. These relationships work well both personally and professionally. Your relationships with people of Star 2, 5, and 8 will be good since Wood controls Earth, and you will be able to receive benefits from your relations with them and be extremely popular. Star 1 people will also be of benefit to you, and you both are likely to hit it off well on a personal level, too.

You need to be cautious around Stars 6 and 7, as these are Metal Stars and they are likely to control your Wood element. With Star 9 people, who are of Fire element, the relationship is likely to start off well but become troubled in the long run, as Fire tends to weaken Wood.

	Compatibility with others Stars (Individuals)	Seek help from this element people or use this sector
Star 3	Stars 2, 5 & 8 (Earth Element)	Fire
	Stars 3 & 4 (wood Element)	Earth
	Stars 6 & 7 (Metal Element)	Water
	Star 9 (Fire Element)	Earth
	Star 1 (Water Element)	Wood

Three Jade Life Star

巽 SE Xun	離 S Li	坤 SW Kun
4 Green WOOD	**9** Purple FIRE	**2** Black EARTH
3 Jade WOOD	**5** Yellow EARTH	**7** Red METAL
8 White EARTH	**1** White WATER	**6** White METAL
艮 NE Gen	坎 N Kan	乾 NW Qian

(Left side: 震 E Zhen; Right side: 兌 W Dui)

The following pages will explain in detail the compatibility factor of a Star 3 person with people of all other nine Stars through the Compatibility Meter. The Compatibility Guides give you tips for managing the relationships in question.

| **3** Jade | compatibility with | **1** White |

Compatibility Meter

When a Star 3 person comes together with a Star 1 person, the result is likely to be mutually fruitful. Star 1 individuals are considerate and caring. They make good business partners because they are extremely driven and creative, coming up with unique solutions to problems. You can trust them to listen to your instructions and get things done without constant oversight. In fact, they thrive when left alone to complete a task! As a natural leader, this is a great asset that you will be able to tap into - you can delegate to Star 1 individuals with peace of mind. They, like you, are impatient, constantly looking for the next thing in life, so they wont drag their feet when deadlines approach! They are very giving and will rarely be short or impatient with you, and as such you feel comfortable around them. You may

find yourself trusting them implicitly because of this and this will make them good choices for friendships and romantic relationships, too. Be aware that they are prone to mood swings and you can, having an intense personality, can be tempted to react to this, escalating problems.

Compatibility Guide

In order to make this connection work, you must not take a Star 1 person for granted. They possess a strong sense of diplomacy which makes them unlikely to directly vocalize problems until an argument erupts! To avoid arguments, listen to their suggestions in the way that they listen to yours and try to take their advice on board instead of always doing things your way. You are straight talking to the point of being rude on occasion and they can take this the wrong way. You may have to curtail your candor when dealing with Star 1 individuals. If you persist in being single-minded and stubborn, the relationship is likely to sour as the both of you will become resentful.

| **3** Jade | compatibility with | **2** Black |

Compatibility Meter

When you and a Star 2 person get together, things may not immediately click. You enjoy being active and you like to plow ahead in all matters. Their patient approach and failure to grasp the urgency of some situations may frustrate you, especially in a business setting where time is money! There is a possibility that you might never become truly close with a Star 2 individual. Yet, on a superficial level where mutual interests are not at stake, there will be an easy camaraderie and attachment that will make for a harmonious connection. In your rare times of need, you can turn to Star 2 individuals. They encourage growth in others and tend to bring out the best in them with their actions. You are naturally inclined to seek out personal growth and so you may benefit

from a friendship with a Star 2 individual in the pursuit of this.

Compatibility Guide

The key to making a connection work with a Star 2 person is to define boundaries and stick to them, as transgressing them will make both of you uncomfortable. Use your instincts to feel out the parameters of the relationship from the start, and then be sure to honor them and treat each other with respect. Star 2 individuals – unlike you – are liable to become submissive and dependent on stronger individuals. They can lose their sense of self and simply go along with everything you do in a relationship or business partnership, and allowing this to happen is unfair on them and unproductive for you. Because they can make themselves so available romantically, you may find yourself becoming bored in the long run unless you can encourage them to retain some independence. You must encourage them to speak their mind as you do, especially when they disagree with you. Respect their differing opinions when they do vocalize them.

| 3 Jade | compatibility with | 3 Jade |

Compatibility Meter

When you and a Star 3 person get together, the results will be quite out of the ordinary! This is because both of you have similar personalities, obviously, and both your personalities are strong ones. You are both happiest when things go your way and you are stubborn and aggressive and passionate. What can make things more problematic is your straight talking which means that any conflict or disagreement will not be put aside and will definitely come to light. You can view this as healthy because it means problems will end up being dealt with directly when two Star 3 people are concerned. In life, small problems frequently grow into bigger ones when left unaddressed, so the tendency for Star 3 individuals to bring up and solve conflict before it is given the

chance to grow can be productive in the long run. If you and another Star 3 individual can get on the same page with a common goal in mind then great progress will be made towards that goal. You can rely on each other whilst still competing for a common interest, keeping things exciting! Clashes and friction keep your relationship interesting which means that you are unlikely to get bored of a Star 3 person in a romantic situation, at least initially.

Compatibility Guide

Conflict will probably be common but short lived. One danger is that you are intense and excitable. You can get into relationships and become too involved initially before realizing your enthusiasm may have been premature and looking elsewhere. Relationships with other people of the same Star, therefore, can be passionate yet short lived. Proceed with caution and a realistic appraisal of the other person so you do not fall head over heels in love, only to get hurt later.

3 Jade compatibility with 4 White

Compatibility Meter

When you and a Star 4 person get together, the relationship is likely to be a good one, especially in terms of their influence on you. Star 4 people will be the type who nurture you and provide you with knowledge. Star 4 people will be attracted to you because of your ability to work hard on your own, and will in their own way find plenty that is admirable and strong in you. They may come to need you and this plays into your natural tendency to lead the way in life and be in control of how things unfold. You will enjoy their dependency to a a degree. You may find it slightly difficult to connect with them on your terms, though. You have a straight laced approach to things, unwavering. It could be said that Star 4 individuals are vague with an often changing opinion on many things. You

might find it hard to "pin them down" because of this which can lead to anger or frustration when you make plans based around them only for them to change their minds.

Compatibility Guide

Some restraint is appropriate in a romantic relationship with Star 4 individuals. Play your cards closer to your chest to pique their interest. Star 4 individuals have a deep love of romance itself and the drama and excitement and mystery that goes with it. Don't spoil this by telling all too easily. On this occasion your straight talking will not serve you well!

3 Jade compatibility with 5 Yellow

Compatibility Meter

When you and a Star 5 person get together, you may get off to a rocky start but if you can get past this then you will likely find yourself enjoying a constructive relationship and one where you will enjoy benefits, in particular if the relationship or partnership is a public one, as they will help boost your reputation and your popularity. The Star 5 person will introduce you to new social connections and help bolster your network. They are a great asset in your efforts to get ahead because they possess more universally accepted social skills and graces than you do, being of the middle ground Star.

Compatibility Guide

It will be important in your relationship with a Star 5 to control your desire for more. In other words, being greedy will likely not work well with them. You cannot seek to control them or become the dominant partner in your interactions because they put great value on being in control and being autonomous. Lacking flexibility in the way they think and being prone to frustration, they could become irritated by your approach to things and vice versa. It is crucial that you learn to work together with them, as both of you can achieve a lot when you have a common goal. Power struggles are a possibility you must be aware of and you will need to ask yourself whether it is more important to have the upper hand or whether it is more important to let the other person have it when it will help achieve a common goal. Give and take! Star 5 individuals are more suited to business partnerships than romantic ones, where friction and disagreement will probably take center stage.

| **3** Jade | compatibility with | **6** White |

Compatibility Meter

When you and a Star 6 person get together, you can expect a complicated dynamic to evolve. Star 6 individuals have a lot of admirable qualities. Their sense of justice and fairness is paramount. As someone who does things by the book, you respect this commitment. Star 6 individuals will have a strong influence on you, and they are likely to shape your personality and moral fiber for the better. However, things can take an interesting turn in the long run. As they are of the Metal Element, and Metal controls Wood, over time they may come to be in control of you – something you are not accustomed to! Obviously this will interfere with your own well laid plans and personal progression. You work best when you are doing things by your own book and problems arise when someone else starts calling the shots.

Compatibility Guide

Although they are not shy by any measure, Star 6 people are known to be deeply private with their feelings, walling themselves off from others. This is the price they pay for living a principled life which often alienates them from everyone else. You are passionate romantically and trying to encourage a Star 6 individual to openly return your feelings may be akin to banging your head off a brick wall. Convincing them to come out of their shell and become a friend or romantic interest is no easy task. Your direct approach may make matters more difficult still, scaring them off! In all matters, keep your expectations realistic, as you may expect more of a Star 6 person than what they're capable of, becoming resentful when they do not achieve at the rate you do.

| **3** Jade | compatibility with | **7** Red |

Compatibility Meter

When you and a Star 7 person come together, the result is hard to call – either things will peter out or they will become quite explosive! You will immediately find yourself interacting easily with this person as they are the most social of the all the Stars, possessing the gift of the gab. All people, including you, are naturally drawn to them socially. Problems may arise in the long term or during times of difficulty when Star 7 individuals, possessing a stormy temperament, are prone to outbursts! Star 7 individuals are known for their sense of pride and arrogance. If you enter into a business partnership with them, over time you will find that they become the decision maker. This is because they are of the Metal element and Metal controls Wood. Your presence may be beneficial to them; your straight talking can help their ego from becoming overinflated

as you will not indulge their narcissism to the same degree that others do. Despite any problem areas in your dynamic, a basic mutual attraction exists between Star 1 and Star 7 and so you will be likely to overcome issues, together. Romantically, you have a compatible world view. You have a passion for life and an innate energy and need to be active which may interact well with Star 7 peoples taste for extravagance and adventure.

Compatibility Guide

If this is a partnership, then you need to put more effort to ensure that things are getting done – instead of relying on the Star 7 person. They are prone to lose their concentration. In a romantic situation they will take the lead if you let them and this will leave you feeling powerless. Remember that they have a strong need for attention and a lack of it will leave them unhappy with you. Don't pander, however. A problem can arise when you try to remain in control of a relationship and they wish to take the reigns. Open communication or sharing of decision making duties may fix this.

| **3** Jade | compatibility with | **8** White |

Compatibility Meter

When you and a Star 8 person come together, the results are perhaps tepid but generally good. This is a good relationship for a partnership, as both of you are able to work closely together for a common interest or cause with minimal conflict. You are likely to enjoy a good public relationship and gain many benefits. There may be plenty of warmth and conviviality, as you have shared principles and goals so much more than interests and pleasures. Being both optimistic when in a positive frame of mind and reliable, you may find that they make good employees or colleagues. Be aware, though, that you will not be able to win a typically unyielding Star 8 individual to your way of thinking if they disagree. They are likely to internalize disagreement and shy away from openly arguing with you, however, which means that they will remain obedient and

dependable in the work place. The potential for difficulty arises when they are your superior at work who has the final say as they can represent a block in your way of your plans!

Compatibility Guide

To make your connection with a Star 8 person work, you will have to be ready to receive and accept constructive suggestions and criticism from the Star 8 person. They very rarely offer suggestions for suggestion's sake, and so whenever they say something it's usually of good use to you, so you will be wise to pay attention and consider carefully what is being said. Being dismissive of their opinions will not advance the relationship or partnership. You must try and encourage them to share their objections and dissenting opinions because otherwise they will be inclined to internalize them instead of articulating them. This will eventually cause problems in all kinds of relationship with a Star 8 individual; romantic, personal or professional. Don't waste your time or become aggressive when you are unable to change their mind.

| **3** Jade | compatibility with | **9** Purple |

Compatibility Meter

When you and a Star 9 person come together, the result is likely to be very good for you initially. Star 9 people are your Noble People, and as such they will offer you lots of education and advice. If you are looking to grow and learn new things then stick around! They tend to be your role models or your mentors, and while all types of relationships are likely to go well, a professional or business relationship in particular will afford you many benefits for your career. Be aware that they may weaken you over time and so you need to make a guarded decision about how intimate you become with them. If you can find a way to keep them at a certain distance whilst still capitalizing on their positive influence then this is advisable.

Compatibility Guide

Whenever you have a problem or have a difficulty to surmount, you will find that a Star 9 person helps you overcome obstacles with ease, leading you to think they might be your guardian angels! You will have very little friction as both of you will get along, but the best way to a lasting relationship is to eliminate differences of opinion (in other words, cultivate understanding). Also, be true to yourself in terms of being sincere and honest – the Star 9 person appreciates this and retaining a strong sense of self will help to negate their slow weakening influence over the long term.

About Joey Yap

Joey Yap first began learning about Chinese Metaphysics from masters in the field when he was fifteen.

Despite having graduated with a Commerce degree in Accounting, Joey never became an accountant. Instead, he began to give seminars, talks and professional Chinese Metaphysic consultations in Malaysia, Singapore, India, Australia, Canada, England, Germany and the United States, becoming a household name in the field.

By the age of twenty-six, Joey became a self-made millionaire and in 2008, he was listed in The Malaysian Tatler as the Top 300 Most Influential People in Malaysia and Prestige's Top 40 Under 40.

His practical and result-driven take on Feng Shui and BaZi sets him apart from other older, traditional masters and practitioners in the field. He shows people how the ancient teachings can be utilized for tangible REAL world benefits. The success he and his clients enjoy, thanks to his advice, is positive proof that Feng Shui and BaZi Astrology works, whether everyone believes in it or not!

Today, Joey has helped and worked with governments and the wealthiest people in Singapore, Hong Kong, China, Malaysia and Japan. His clients include multinationals, developers, tycoons and royalties. On Bloomberg, he is featured on-air as a regular guest on the subject of Feng Shui annual forecasts. He is retained by twenty-five top Malaysian property developers to help determine suitable candidates to take top management, change their space and Feng Shui mechanism, the way they make decisions, and understand the natural cosmic energies that can influence their decision-making.

Every year he conducts his 'Feng Shui and Astrology' seminar to a crowd of more than 3500 people at the Kuala Lumpur Convention Center. He also takes this annual seminar on a world tour to Frankfurt, San Francisco, New York, Las Vegas, Toronto, Sydney and Singapore.

The Joey Yap Consulting Group is the world's largest and first specialized metaphysics consultation firm. His consultancy, and professional speaking and training engagements with Microsoft, HP, Bloomberg, Citibank, HSBC and many more have seen the benefits of Classical Feng Shui and BaZi find their way into corporate environment and culture. Celebrities, property developers and other large organizations turn to Joey when they need the best.

After years of field-testing and fine-tuning his teachings, he has put together a team in the form of Joey Yap Research International. The objective of this Research Team is to scientifically track and verify the positive impact of Feng Shui and BaZi on subjects and ultimately to assist more people in achieving their life goals.

The Mastery Academy of Chinese Metaphysics which Joey founded teaches thousands of students from all around the world about Classical Feng Shui, Chinese Astrology and Face Reading. Many graduates have gone on to become successful in their own right, becoming sought after consultants, setting up their own consultancy businesses or even becoming educators, passing on Chinese Metaphysics knowledge to others.

Joey has also created the Decision Referential Technology™, offering decision reformation training on how to make better decisions in business and in personal life. He has led his team of highly trained consultants to help clients create more positive change in corporate boardrooms and increase production in their companies, helping people see their business outlook for each year so they may anticipate, plan and execute their strategies successfully.

Joey's work has been featured regularly in various popular global publications and networks like Time, Forbes, the International Herald Tribune and Bloomberg. He has also written columns for The New Straits Times, The Star and The Edge – Malaysia's leading newspapers. He has achieved bestselling author status with over sixty-five books, which have sold more than three million copies to-date.

His success is not limited to matters of Feng Shui and BaZi. Although his success is a product of them, he is also a successful entrepreneur, leading his own companies and property investment portfolio. When not teaching metaphysics or consulting around the world, Joey is a Naruto-fan, avid snowboarder and is crazy for fruits de mer.

Author's personal website :

 www.joeyyap.com

Joey Yap on Facebook:

 www.facebook.com/JoeyYapFB

www.masteryacademy.com | +603 - 2284 8080

MASTERY ACADEMY
OF CHINESE METAPHYSICS
Your **Preferred** Choice to the Art & Science of
Classical Chinese Metaphysics Studies

Bringing **innovative** techniques and **creative** teaching methods to an ancient study.

Mastery Academy of Chinese Metaphysics was established by Joey Yap to play the role of disseminating this Eastern knowledge to the modern world with the belief that this valuable knowledge should be accessible to anyone, anywhere.

Its goal is to enrich people's lives through accurate, professional teaching and practice of Chinese Metaphysics knowledge globally. It is the first academic institution of its kind in the world to adopt the tradition of Western institutions of higher learning - where students are encourage to explore, question and challenge themselves and to respect different fields and branches of study - with the appreciation and respect of classical ideas and applications that have stood the test of time.

The art and science of Chinese Metaphysics studies – be it Feng Shui, BaZi (Astrology), Mian Xiang (Face Reading), ZeRi (Date Selection) or Yi Jing – is no longer a field shrouded with mystery and superstition. In light of new technology, fresher interpretations and innovative methods as well as modern teaching tools like the Internet, interactive learning, e-learning and distance learning, anyone from virtually any corner of the globe, who is keen to master these disciplines can do so with ease and confidence under the guidance and support of the Academy.

It has indeed proven to be a center of educational excellence for thousands of students from over thirty countries across the world; many of whom have moved on to practice classical Chinese Metaphysics professionally in their home countries.

At the Academy, we believe in enriching people's lives by empowering their destinies through the disciplines of Chinese Metaphysics. Learning is not an option - it's a way of life!

MASTERY ACADEMY
OF CHINESE METAPHYSICS™

MALAYSIA
19-3, The Boulevard, Mid Valley City, 59200 Kuala Lumpur, Malaysia
Tel : +603-2284 8080 | Fax : +603-2284 1218
Email   : info@masteryacademy.com
Website : www.masteryacademy.com

Australia, Austria, Canada, China, Croatia, Cyprus, Czech Republic, Denmark, France, Germany, Greece, Hungary, India, Italy, Kazakhstan, Malaysia, Netherlands (Holland), New Zealand, Philippines, Poland, Russian Federation, Singapore, Slovenia, South Africa, Switzerland, Turkey, U.S.A., Ukraine, United Kingdom

JOEY YAP CONSULTING GROUP

Pioneering Metaphysics - Centric Personal Coaching and Corporate Consulting

The Joey Yap Consulting Group is the world's first specialised metaphysics consultation firm. Founded in 2002 by renown international Feng Shui and BaZi consultant, author and trainer Joey Yap, the Joey Yap Consulting Group is a pioneer in the provision of metaphysics-driven coaching and consultation services for individuals and corporations.

The Group's core consultation practice areas are Feng Shui and BaZi, which are complimented by ancillary services like Date Selection, Face Reading and Yi Jing Divination. The Group's team of highly-trained professional consultants are led by Principal Consultant Joey Yap. The Joey Yap Consulting Group is the firm of choice for corporate captains, entrepreneurs, celebrities and property developers when it comes to Feng Shui and BaZi-related advisory and knowledge.

Across Industries: Our Portfolio of Clients

Our diverse portfolio of both corporate and individual clients from all around the world bears testimony to our experience and capabilities.

Joey Yap Consulting Group is the firm of choice for many of Asia's leading multi-national corporations, listed entities, conglomerates and top-tier property developers when it comes to Feng Shui and corporate BaZi.

Our services also engaged by professionals, prominent business personalities, celebrities, high-profile politicians and people from all walks of life.

JOEY YAP CONSULTING GROUP

Name (Mr./Mrs./Ms.):_____

Contact Details

Tel:_____ Fax:_____

Mobile :_____

E-mail:_____

What Type of Consultation Are You Interested In?
☐ Feng Shui   ☐ BaZi   ☐ Date Selection   ☐ Corporate Events

Please tick if applicable:
☐ Are you a Property Developer looking to engage Joey Yap Consulting Group?

☐ Are you a Property Investor looking for tailor-made packages to suit your investment requirements?

Please attach your name card here.

Thank you for completing this form. Please fax it back to us at:

Malaysia & the rest of the world
Fax : +603-2284 2213   Tel : +603-2284 1213

www.joeyyap.com

Feng Shui Consultations

For Residential Properties
- Initial Land/Property Assessment
- Residential Feng Shui Consultations
- Residential Land Selection
- End-to-End Residential Consultation

For Commercial Properties
- Initial Land/Property Assessment
- Commercial Feng Shui Consultations
- Commercial Land Selection
- End-to-End Commercial Consultation

For Property Developers
- End-to-End Consultation
- Post-Consultation Advisory Services
- Panel Feng Shui Consultant

For Property Investors
- Your Personal Feng Shui Consultant
- Tailor-Made Packages

For Memorial Parks & Burial Sites
- Yin House Feng Shui

BaZi Consultations

Personal Destiny Analysis
- Personal Destiny Analysis for Individuals
- Children's BaZi Analysis
- Family BaZi Analysis

Strategic Analysis for Corporate Organizations
- Corporate BaZi Consultations
- BaZi Analysis for Human Resource Management

Entrepreneurs & Business Owners
- BaZi Analysis for Entrepreneurs

Career Pursuits
- BaZi Career Analysis

Relationships
- Marriage and Compatibility Analysis
- Partnership Analysis

For Everyone
- Annual BaZi Forecast
- Your Personal BaZi Coach

Date Selection Consultations

- **Marriage Date Selection**
- **Caesarean Birth Date Selection**
- **House-Moving Date Selection**
- **Renovation & Groundbreaking Dates**
- **Signing of Contracts**
- **Official Openings**
- **Product Launches**

Corporate Events

Many reputable organizations and instituitions have worked closely with Joey Yap Consulting Group to build a synergistic business relationship by engaging our team of consultants, led by Joey Yap, as speakers at their corporate events.

We tailor our seminars and talks to suit the anticipated or pertinent group of audience. Be it department, subsidiary, your clients or even the entire corporation, we aim to fit your requirements in delivering the intended message(s).

Tel: +603-2284 1213   Email: consultation@joeyyap.com

CHINESE METAPHYSICS REFERENCE SERIES

The Chinese Metaphysics Reference Series is a collection of reference texts, source material, and educational textbooks to be used as supplementary guides by scholars, students, researchers, teachers and practitioners of Chinese Metaphysics.

These comprehensive and structured books provide fast, easy reference to aid in the study and practice of various Chinese Metaphysics subjects including Feng Shui, BaZi, Yi Jing, Zi Wei, Liu Ren, Ze Ri, Ta Yi, Qi Men and Mian Xiang.

The Chinese Metaphysics Compendium

At over 1,000 pages, the *Chinese Metaphysics Compendium* is a unique one-volume reference book that compiles all the formulas relating to Feng Shui, BaZi (Four Pillars of Destiny), Zi Wei (Purple Star Astrology), Yi Jing (I-Ching), Qi Men (Mystical Doorways), Ze Ri (Date Selection), Mian Xiang (Face Reading) and other sources of Chinese Metaphysics.

It is presented in the form of easy-to-read tables, diagrams and reference charts, all of which are compiled into one handy book. This first-of-its-kind compendium is presented in both English and the original Chinese, so that none of the meanings and contexts of the technical terminologies are lost.

The only essential and comprehensive reference on Chinese Metaphysics, and an absolute must-have for all students, scholars, and practitioners of Chinese Metaphysics.

The Ten Thousand Year Calendar (Pocket Edition)

The Ten Thousand Year Calendar

Dong Gong Date Selection

The Date Selection Compendium

Plum Blossoms Divination Reference Book

San Yuan Dragon Gate Eight Formations Water Method

Xuan Kong Da Gua Ten Thousand Year Calendar

Bazi Hour Pillar Useful Gods - Wood

Bazi Hour Pillar Useful Gods - Fire

Bazi Hour Pillar Useful Gods - Earth

Bazi Hour Pillar Useful Gods - Metal

Bazi Hour Pillar Useful Gods - Water

Xuan Kong Da Gua Structures Reference Book

Xuan Kong Da Gua 64 Gua Transformation Analysis

Bazi Structures and Structural Useful Gods - Wood

Bazi Structures and Structural Useful Gods - Fire

Bazi Structures and Structural Useful Gods - Earth

Bazi Structures and Structural Useful Gods - Metal

Bazi Structures and Structural Useful Gods - Water

Xuan Kong Purple White Script

Earth Study Discern Truth Second Edition

---

www.masteryacademy.com | +603 - 2284 8080

Joey Yap's BaZi Profiling System

Three Levels of BaZi Profiling (English & Chinese versions)

In BaZi Profiling, there are three levels that reflect three different stages of a person's personal nature and character structure.

Level 1 – The Day Master

The Day Master in a nutshell is the BASIC YOU. The inborn personality. It is your essential character. It answers the basic question "WHO AM I". There are ten basic personality profiles – the TEN Day Masters – each with its unique set of personality traits, likes and dislikes.

Level 2 – The Structure

The Structure is your behavior and attitude – in other words, how you use your personality. It expands on the Day Master (Level 1). The structure reveals your natural tendencies in life – are you more controlling, more of a creator, supporter, thinker or connector? Each of the Ten Day Masters express themselves differently through the FIVE Structures. Why do we do the things we do? Why do we like the things we like? – The answers are in our BaZi STRUCTURE.

Level 3 – The Profile

The Profile reveals your unique abilities and skills, the masks that you consciously and unconsciously "put on" as you approach and navigate the world. Your Profile speaks of your ROLES in life. There are TEN roles – or Ten BaZi Profiles. Everyone plays a different role.

What makes you happy and what does success mean to you is different to somebody else. Your sense of achievement and sense of purpose in life is unique to your Profile. Your Profile will reveal your unique style.

The path of least resistance to your success and wealth can only be accessed once you get into your "flow." Your BaZi Profile reveals how you can get FLOW. It will show you your patterns in work, relationship and social settings. Being AWARE of these patterns is your first step to positive Life Transformation.

www.baziprofiling.com

BaZi Collections

Leading Chinese Astrology Master Trainer Joey Yap makes it easy to learn how to unlock your Destiny through your BaZi with these books. BaZi or Four Pillars of Destiny is an ancient Chinese science which enables individuals to understand their personality, hidden talents and abilities as well as their luck cycle, simply by examining the information contained within their birth data.

Understand and appreciate more about this astoundingly accurate ancient Chinese Metaphysical science with this BaZi Collection.

Feng Shui Collection

Must-Haves for Property Analysis!

For homeowners, those looking to build their own home or even investors who are looking to apply Feng Shui to their homes, these series of books provides valuable information from the classical Feng Shui therioes and applications.

In his trademark straight-to-the-point manner, Joey shares with you the Feng Shui do's and dont's when it comes to finding a property with favorable Feng Shui, which is condusive for home living.

Stories & Lessons on Feng Shui Series

All in all, this series is a delightful chronicle of Joey's articles, thoughts and vast experience - as a professional Feng Shui consultant and instructor - that have been purposely refined, edited and expanded upon to make for a light-hearted, interesting yet educational read. And with Feng Shui, BaZi, Mian Xiang and Yi Jing all thrown into this one dish, there's something for everyone.

www.masteryacademy.com | +603 - 2284 8080

Continue Your Journey with Joey Yap Books in Feng Shui

Pure Feng Shui
Pure Feng Shui is Joey Yap's debut with an international publisher, CICO Books, and is a refreshing and elegant look at the intricacies of Classical Feng Shui – now compiled in a useful manner for modern-day readers. This book is a comprehensive introduction to all the important precepts and techniques of Feng Shui practice.

Your Aquarium Here
This book is the first in Fengshuilogy Series, a series of matter-in-fact and useful Feng Shui books designed for the person who wants to do a fuss-free Feng Shui.

Xuan Kong Flying Stars
This book is an essential introductory book to the subject of Xuan Kong Fei Xing, a well-known and popular system of Feng Shui. Learn 'tricks of the trade' and 'trade secrets' to enhance and maximize Qi in your home or office.

Walking the Dragons
Compiled in one book for the first time from Joey Yap's Feng Shui Mastery Excursion Series, the book highlights China's extensive, vibrant history with astute observations on the Feng Shui of important sites and places. Learn the landform formations of Yin Houses (tombs and burial places), as well as mountains, temples, castles, and villages.

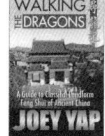

The Art of Date Selection: Personal Date Selection
With the *Art of Date Selection: Personal Date Selection*, learn simple, practical methods you can employ to select not just good dates, but personalized good dates. Whether it's a personal activity such as a marriage or professional endeavor such as launching a business, signing a contract or even acquiring assets, this book will show you how to pick the good dates and tailor them to suit the activity in question, as well as avoid the negative ones too!

www.masteryacademy.com | +603 - 2284 8080

Face Reading Collection

Discover Face Reding (English & Chinese versions)

This is a comprehensive book on all areas of Face Reading, covering some of the most important facial features, including the forehead, mouth, ears and even philtrum above your lips. This book eill help you analyse not just your Destiny but help you achieve your full potential and achieve life fulfillment.

Joey Yap's Art of Face Reading

The Art of Face Reading is Joey Yap's second effort with CICO Books, and takes a lighter, more practical approach to Face Reading. This book does not so much focus on the individual features as it does on reading the entire face. It is about identifying common personality types and characters.

Easy Guide on Face Reading (English & Chinese versions)

The Face Reading Essentials series of books comprises 5 individual books on the key features of the face – Eyes, Eyebrows, Ears, Nose, and Mouth. Each book provides a detailed illustration and a simple yet descriptive explanation on the individual types of the features.

The books are equally useful and effective for beginners, enthusiasts, and the curious. The series is designed to enable people who are new to Face Reading to make the most of first impressions and learn to apply Face Reading skills to understand the personality and character of friends, family, co-workers, and even business associates.

Annual Releases
2011 Annual Outlook & Tong Shu

Chinese Astrology for 2011   Feng Shui for 2011   Tong Shu Desktop Calendar 2011   Professional Tong Shu Diary 2011   Tong Shu Monthly Planner 2011   Weekly Tong Shu Diary 2011

www.masteryacademy.com | +603 - 2284 8080

Educational Tools and Software

Xuan Kong Flying Stars Feng Shui Software
The Essential Application for Enthusiasts and Professionals

The Xuan Kong Flying Stars Feng Shui Software will assist you in the practice of Xuan Kong Feng Shui with minimum fuss and maximum effectiveness. Superimpose the Flying Stars charts over your house plans (or those of your clients) to clearly demarcate the 9 Palaces. Use it to help you create fast and sophisticated chart drawings and presentations, as well as to assist professional practitioners in the report-writing process before presenting the final reports for your clients. Students can use it to practice their Xuan Kong Feng Shui skills and knowledge, and it can even be used by designers and architects!

BaZi Ming Pan Software Version 2.0
Professional Four Pillars Calculator for Destiny Analysis

The BaZi Ming Pan Version 2.0 Professional Four Pillars Calculator for Destiny Analysis is the most technically advanced software of its kind in the world today. It allows even those without any knowledge of BaZi to generate their own BaZi Charts, and provides virtually every detail required to undertake a comprehensive Destiny Analysis.

This Professional Four Pillars Calculator allows you to even undertake a day-to-day analysis of your Destiny. What's more, all BaZi Charts generated by this software are fully printable and configurable! Designed for both enthusiasts and professional practitioners, this state-of-the-art software blends details with simplicity, and is capable of generating 4 different types of BaZi charts: **BaZi Professional Charts, BaZi Annual Analysis Charts, BaZi Pillar Analysis Charts and BaZi Family Relationship Charts.**

Joey Yap Feng Shui Template Set

Directions are the cornerstone of any successful Feng Shui audit or application. The **Joey Yap Feng Shui Template Set** is a set of three templates to simplify the process of taking directions and determining locations and positions, whether it's for a building, a house, or an open area such as a plot of land, all with just a floor plan or area map.

The Set comprises 3 basic templates: The Basic Feng Shui Template, 8 Mansions Feng Shui Template, and the Flying Stars Feng Shui Template.

Mini Feng Shui Compass

The Mini Feng Shui Compass is a self-aligning compass that is not only light at 100gms but also built sturdily to ensure it will be convenient to use anywhere. The rings on the Mini Feng Shui Compass are bi-lingual and incorporate the 24 Mountain Rings that is used in your traditional Luo Pan.

The comprehensive booklet included will guide you in applying the 24 Mountain Directions on your Mini Feng Shui Compass effectively and the 8 Mansions Feng Shui to locate the most auspicious locations within your home, office and surroundings. You can also use the Mini Feng Shui Compass when measuring the direction of your property for the purpose of applying Flying Stars Feng Shui.

www.masteryacademy.com | +603 - 2284 8080

Educational Tools and Software

Xuan Kong Vol.1
An Advanced Feng Shui Home Study Course

Learn the Xuan Kong Flying Star Feng Shui system in just 20 lessons! Joey Yap's specialised notes and course work have been written to enable distance learning without compromising on the breadth or quality of the syllabus. Learn at your own pace with the same material students in a live class would use. The most comprehensive distance learning course on Xuan Kong Flying Star Feng Shui in the market. Xuan Kong Flying Star Vol.1 comes complete with a special binder for all your course notes.

Feng Shui for Period 8 - (DVD)

Don't miss the Feng Shui Event of the next 20 years! Catch Joey Yap LIVE and find out just what Period 8 is all about. This DVD boxed set zips you through the fundamentals of Feng Shui and the impact of this important change in the Feng Shui calendar. Joey's entertaining, conversational style walks you through the key changes that Period 8 will bring and how to tap into Wealth Qi and Good Feng Shui for the next 20 years.

Xuan Kong Flying Stars Beginners Workshop - (DVD)

Take a front row seat in Joey Yap's Xuan Kong Flying Stars workshop with this unique LIVE RECORDING of Joey Yap's Xuan Kong Flying Stars Feng Shui workshop, attended by over 500 people. This DVD program provides an effective and quick introduction of Xuan Kong Feng Shui essentials for those who are just starting out in their study of classical Feng Shui. Learn to plot your own Flying Star chart in just 3 hours. Learn 'trade secret' methods, remedies and cures for Flying Stars Feng Shui. This boxed set contains 3 DVDs and 1 workbook with notes and charts for reference.

BaZi Four Pillars of Destiny Beginners Workshop - (DVD)

Ever wondered what Destiny has in store for you? Or curious to know how you can learn more about your personality and inner talents? BaZi or Four Pillars of Destiny is an ancient Chinese science that enables us to understand a person's hidden talent, inner potential, personality, health and wealth luck from just their birth data. This specially compiled DVD set of Joey Yap's BaZi Beginners Workshop provides a thorough and comprehensive introduction to BaZi. Learn how to read your own chart and understand your own luck cycle. This boxed set contains 3 DVDs and 1 workbook with notes and reference charts.

www.masteryacademy.com | +603 - 2284 8080

DVD Series

Joey Yap's Face Reading Revealed DVD Series

Mian Xiang, the Chinese art of Face Reading, is an ancient form of physiognomy and entails the use of the face and facial characteristics to evaluate key aspects of a person's life, luck and destiny. In his Face Reading DVDs series, Joey Yap shows you how the facial features reveal a wealth of information about a person's luck, destiny and personality.

Mian Xiang also tell us the talents, quirks and personality of an individual. Do you know that just by looking at a person's face, you can ascertain his or her health, wealth, relationships and career? Let Joey Yap show you how the 12 Palaces can be utilised to reveal a person's inner talents, characteristics and much more.

Feng Shui for Homebuyers DVD Series

In these DVDs, you will also learn how to identify properties with good Feng Shui features that will help you promote a fulfilling life and achieve your full potential. Discover how to avoid properties with negative Feng Shui that can bring about detrimental effects to your health, wealth and relationships.

Joey will also elaborate on how to fix the various aspects of your home that may have an impact on the Feng Shui of your property and give pointers on how to tap into the positive energies to support your goals.

Discover Feng Shui with Joey Yap: Set of 4 DVDs
Informative and entertaining, classical Feng Shui comes alive in *Discover Feng Shui with Joey Yap!*

You have the questions. Now let Joey personally answer them in this 4-set DVD compilation! Learn how to ensure the viability of your residence or workplace, Feng Shui-wise, without having to convert it into a Chinese antiques' shop. Classical Feng Shui is about harnessing the natural power of your environment to improve quality of life. It's a systematic and subtle metaphysical science.

Walking the Dragons with Joey Yap (The TV Series)

This DVD set features eight episodes, covering various landform Feng Shui analyses and applications from Joey Yap as he and his co-hosts travel through China. It includes case studies of both modern and historical sites with a focus on Yin House (burial places) Feng Shui and the tombs of the Qing Dynasty emperors.

The series was partly filmed on-location in mainland China, and the state of Selangor, Malaysia.

www.masteryacademy.com | +603 - 2284 8080

Home Study Courses

Gain Valuable Knowledge from the Comfort of Your Home

Now, armed with your trusty computer or laptop and Internet access, knowledge of Chinese Metaphysics is just a click away!

3 easy steps to activate your Home Study Course:

Step 1:
Go to the URL as indicated on the Activation Card, and key in your Activation Code

Step 2:
At the Registration page, fill in the details accordingly to enable us to generate your Student Identification (Student ID).

Step 3:
Upon successful registration, you may begin your lessons immediately.

Joey Yap's Feng Shui Mastery HomeStudy Course

Module 1: **Empowering Your Home**
Module 2: **Master Practitioner Program**

Learn how easy it is to harness the power of the environment to promote health, wealth and prosperity in your life. The knowledge and applications of Feng Shui will no more be a mystery but a valuable tool you can master on your own.

Joey Yap's BaZi Mastery HomeStudy Course

Module 1: **Mapping Your Life**
Module 2: **Mastering Your Future**

Discover your path of least resistance to success with insights about your personality and capabilities, and what strengths you can tap on to maximize your potential for success and happiness by mastering BaZi (Chinese Astrology). This course will teach you all the essentials you need to interpret a BaZi chart and more.

Joey Yap's Mian Xiang Mastery HomeStudy Course

Module 1: **Face Reading**
Module 2: **Advanced Face Reading**

A face can reveal so much about a person. Now, you can learn the art and science of Mian Xiang (Chinese Face Reading) to understand a person's character based on his or her facial features with ease and confidence.

www.masteryacademy.com | +603 - 2284 8080

Feng Shui Mastery™
LIVE COURSES (MODULES ONE TO FOUR)

The Feng Shui Mastery™ comprises Feng Shui Mastery Modules 1, 2, 3 and 4. It starts off with a foundation program up to the advanced practitioner level. It is a thorough, comprehensive program that covers important theories from various classical Feng Shui systems including Ba Zhai, San Yuan, San He, and Xuan Kong.

Module One: Beginners Course   **Module Two:** Practitioners Course   **Module Three:** Advanced Practitioners Course   **Module Four:** Master Course

BaZi Mastery™
LIVE COURSES (MODULES ONE TO FOUR)

The BaZi Mastery™ consists of BaZi Mastery Modules 1, 2, 3 and 4. In Modules 1 and 2, students will receive a thorough introduction to BaZi, along with an intensive understanding of BaZi principles and the requisite skills to practice it with accuracy and precision. This will prepare them, and serious Feng Shui practitioners, for a more advanced levels and fine-tune their application skills in Modules 3 and 4.

Module One: Intensive Foundation Course   **Module Two:** Practitioners Course   **Module Three:** Advanced Practitioners Course   **Module Four:** Master Course in BaZi

XUAN KONG MASTERY™
LIVE COURSES (MODULES ONE TO THREE)
*Advanced Courses For Master Practitioners

The Xuan Kong Mastery™ comprises Xuan Kong Mastery Modules 1, 2A, 2B and 3. It is a sophisticated branch of Feng Shui replete with many techniques and formulae, enabling practitioners to evaluate Feng Shui on a more thorough and in-depth basis. The study of Xuan Kong encompasses numerology, symbology and science of the Ba Gua along with the mathematics of time.

Module One: Advanced Foundation Course   **Module Two A:** Advanced Xuan Kong Methodologies   **Module Two B:** Purple White   **Module Three:** Advanced Xuan Kong Da Gua

www.masteryacademy.com | +603 - 2284 8080

Mian Xiang Mastery™
LIVE COURSES (MODULES ONE AND TWO)

The Mian Xiang Mastery™ comprises of Mian Xiang Mastery Modules 1 and 2 to allow students to learn this ancient art in a thorough, detailed manner. Each module has a carefully-developed syllabus that allows students to get acquainted with the fundamentals of Mian Xiang before moving on to the more intricate theories and principles that will enable them to practice Mian Xiang with greater depth and complexity.

Module One:
Basic Face Reading

Module Two:
Practical Face Reading

Yi Jing Mastery™
LIVE COURSES (MODULES ONE AND TWO)

The Yi Jing Mastery™ comprises Modules 1 and 2. Both Modules aim to give casual and serious Yi Jing enthusiasts a serious insight into one of the most important philosophical treatises in ancient Chinese thought. Yi Jing uses sophisticated formulas and calculations to derive the answers to questions we pose. It is a science of divination, and in our classes there is a heavy emphasis on the scientific aspect of it. It bears no religious or superstitious affiliation.

Module One:
Traditional Yi Jing

Module Two:
Plum Blossom Numerology

Ze Ri Mastery™
LIVE COURSES (MODULES ONE AND TWO)

The ZeRi Mastery™ consists of ZeRi Mastery Modules 1 and 2. This program provides students with a thorough introduction to the art of Date Selection both for Personal and Feng Shui purposes. Our ZeRi Mastery™ aims to provide a thorough and comprehensive program on the art of Date Selection, covering everything from Personal and Feng Shui Date Selection to Xuan Kong Da Gua Date Selection.

Module One:
Personal and Feng Shui Date Selection

Module Two:
Xuan Kong Da Gua Date Selection

www.masteryacademy.com | +603 - 2284 8080

Feng Shui for Life

This is an entry-level five-day course designed for the Feng Shui beginner to learn the application of practical Feng Shui in day-to-day living. Lessons include quick tips on analyzing the BaZi chart, simple Feng Shui solutions for the home, basic Date Selection, useful Face Reading techniques and practical Water formulas. A great introduction course on Chinese Metaphysics studies for beginners.

Joey Yap's
Design Your Destiny

This is a three-day life transformation program designed to inspire awareness and action for you to create a better quality of life. It introduces the DRT™ (Decision Referential Technology) method, which utilizes the BaZi Personality Profiling system to determine the right version of you, and serves as a tool to help you make better decisions and achieve a better life in the least resistant way possible based on your Personality Profile Type.

Walk the Mountains! Learn Feng Shui in a Practical and Hands-on Program

 ### Feng Shui Mastery Excursion™

Learn landform (Luan Tou) Feng Shui by walking the mountains and chasing the Dragon's vein in China. This Program takes the students in a study tour to examine notable Feng Shui landmarks, mountains, hills, valleys, ancient palaces, famous mansions, houses and tombs in China. The Excursion is a 'practical' hands-on course where students are shown to perform readings using the formulas they've learnt and to recognize and read Feng Shui Landform (Luan Tou) formations.

Read about China Excursion here:
http://www.fengshuiexcursion.com

> Mastery Academy courses are conducted around the world. Find out when will Joey Yap be in your area by visiting **www.masteryacademy.com** or call our office at **+603-2284 8080**.

www.masteryacademy.com | +603 - 2284 8080